Start Investing in ETFs

Start Investing in ETFs

How to diversify smartly with low-cost, high-impact exchange-traded funds

Julian Raye

Mindful Pages

Published in 2025

ISBN: 9789371779821 (PB)
ISBN: 9789371773164 (eBook)

Published by

Mindful Pages
Imprint of Alpha Editions LLC
312 W. 2nd St #1834
Casper, WY 82601, USA

This book was developed using advanced writing tools to support the drafting and ideation process. All content has been thoughtfully curated, refined, and reviewed to ensure quality and relevance.

Content

Introduction
The Quiet Revolution of Intelligent Investing

There is a curious paradox at the heart of modern finance. Never before have ordinary investors had such unprecedented access to information, yet few have felt more uncertain. Markets speak in a relentless hum—news tickers scroll endlessly, pundits proclaim certainty from contradictory data, and social media amplifies the slightest tremor into a cacophony of fear. The result is a culture that often rewards noise over insight, impulse over deliberation.

This book is not for those content to drift within that chaos. *Start Investing in ETFs* is for readers who suspect—sometimes quietly, sometimes urgently—that a calmer approach is possible. Investing need not be a frenetic performance, a string of speculative stunts, or a desperate attempt to outpace the next downturn. Money can be managed not through constant motion, but with considered composure. The markets are not a casino; they are a mechanism that can be navigated with clarity, confidence, and grace.

At the centre of this disciplined approach is a tool often underappreciated: the exchange-traded fund. This book treats ETFs not merely as financial products, but as instruments of intentionality—modular, efficient, and elegant structures that allow investors to build portfolios with coherence and purpose. Here, an ETF is not simply convenient; it is a framework for a smarter, more grounded relationship with capital.

This is not another tome promising that you will "beat the market." Such promises are fleeting and often accidental. Instead, we offer something more enduring: a method to stop outguessing the system and begin constructing within it. The emphasis is not prediction, but design. Not bravado, but clarity. Not spectacle, but substance.

From Chaos to Composition

Modern investing culture prizes short-termism. The next hot stock, the latest innovation, the boldest forecast—these are constantly presented as imperatives. Financial media packages speculation as insight, and volatility as opportunity. The result is performative investing: activity mistaken for progress, even among intelligent actors, who may act irrationally when faced with uncertainty.

The data, however, tells a consistent story. Most active investors underperform the market over time. This is rarely due to a lack of intellect or diligence; it is because the system resists perfect timing and flawless foresight. Quiet, empirical evidence shows that simplicity, especially when paired with consistency and cost discipline, often triumphs over complexity.

ETFs exemplify this simplicity at scale. Through a single, low-cost transaction, they provide exposure to broad swathes of the global economy. Transparent and efficient, they are built to be held rather than traded. When used judiciously, they offer diversification without confusion, strategy without speculation.

Of course, ETFs are not inherently superior to all other instruments, nor are they infallible. Their effectiveness depends on the hands that wield them. Yet in the grasp of an intentional investor, they become more than products—they become building blocks for a thoughtful financial life.

What This Book Is—and Isn't

This book does not catalogue fund recommendations or present market predictions disguised as wisdom. It will not tell you what to buy next Tuesday or which sector is "poised to explode" this year. That language belongs to gambling, not investing.

Instead, it offers a grounded philosophy of ownership. We begin by confronting myths about stock picking, market timing, and the illusion of control. We explore the structure of ETFs themselves:

how they function, why they exist, and how they differ from mutual funds or individual equities. We examine the psychological pitfalls that ensnare even informed investors, and the power of behavioural design to counteract them.

From there, we explore how to choose ETFs thoughtfully, how to construct portfolios aligned with financial goals and emotional resilience, and how to assess progress in ways that complement a meaningful life rather than a spreadsheet. Finally, we consider investing as a moral and philosophical act: how your portfolio reflects your values and the world you wish to inhabit.

This is not a technical manual alone. It is a call for discipline, a case for reflection, a manifesto for clarity.

Why This Matters Now

The urgency of this message is unmistakable. Financial markets have never been more accessible—apps allow trades at a swipe, algorithms recommend complex products instantly—yet confusion has deepened. Investors are overinformed, underprepared. They possess data, but not wisdom; facts, but not frameworks.

Economic cycles have accelerated, geopolitical shocks are frequent, and trust in institutions is fragile. In this context, a passive, diversified ETF portfolio may seem almost quaint. Yet this simplicity is no naïve shortcut; it reflects intellectual rigour and historical evidence. Over decades, investing has always been about participation rather than prediction. ETFs offer one of the most reliable, low-cost means to partake meaningfully in the world's economic growth. They allow investors to build wealth through structure, not spectacle.

The Investor You Become

Long-term investing cultivates character: patience, rationality, groundedness. These are not merely financial virtues—they are human ones. A disciplined investor becomes a more deliberate thinker: less reactive, more reflective; less impulsive, more intentional.

This book honours that mindset. It assumes you seek systems rather than shortcuts, clarity rather than secrets, reflection rather than speed. The goal is not solely asset growth, but the construction of a coherent financial life—anchored in timeless principles rather than transient forecasts, in thoughtful practice rather than noisy reaction.

A Final Word Before We Begin

If investing has left you overwhelmed, you are not alone. If prior plans have faltered, it is not failure; it is the system at work, designed to provoke doubt and reward distraction. What this book offers is a new lens: to see investing as stewardship rather than speculation.

Mechanics are important, yes—but mindset is paramount. You will learn to resist the pull of constant chasing, to prize simplicity over spectacle, and to recognise that peace of mind is itself a return worth pursuing.

The chapters ahead provide structure, insight, and practical guidance. But above all, this introduction serves as a reminder: you do not need to join the noisy fray. There is a quieter revolution in investing, unfolding one portfolio, one investor at a time.

Let us begin.

Chapter 1
What Are You Really Buying? A Philosophy of Ownership

Investing often begins with a whisper—a company name, a ticker, a tip overheard in a corridor or amplified across social media. There is a peculiar thrill in imagining that we might glimpse what others cannot, anticipate a rise before it arrives, or sidestep a collapse just in time. Markets entice with the notion that secrets lie hidden, waiting for those nimble and attentive enough to uncover them. Yet decades of evidence tell a far less romantic story: this kind of foresight is not merely rare—it is largely illusory.

Ownership in today's financial world is rarely tangible. We purchase symbols—abstract representations of businesses, sectors, or economies—often without pausing to ask a fundamental question: what am I truly acquiring? This chapter returns that question to the centre of intelligent investing.

We start by dismantling the myth of the market whisperer—the enduring belief that some individuals or strategies can consistently outpace the collective intelligence of markets. This notion persists not because it is accurate, but because it comforts. It offers an illusion of control in a system defined by uncertainty. In truth, the majority of active investors underperform their benchmarks, frequently not in spite of their effort, but because of it. The obstacle is not ambition or intellect—it is the human tendency to mistake randomness for signal, volatility for opportunity, and activity for progress.

Cognitive science has catalogued these pitfalls: overconfidence bias, loss aversion, anchoring, the recency effect. These are not shortcomings of the uninformed; they are intrinsic to human psychology, reinforced by a financial ecosystem that thrives on movement, commentary, and churn. Modern investors do not merely compete with the market—they contend with their own neurochemistry, primed for impulsivity in a context that rewards patience. The myth of the market whisperer is therefore as much about identity as strategy: it flatters us into believing that insight drives success, when often it is design that does.

If prediction is unreliable, what remains? The answer lies in ownership—real, deliberate, structured ownership. Not of stories or trends, but of systems. This is where the ETF emerges as a tool of philosophical as well as financial clarity.

Too often dismissed as bland, ETFs are far more than the sum of their parts. They are modular expressions of worldview. Buying an S&P 500 ETF is a tacit endorsement of American corporate resilience. Investing in a global all-cap index conveys belief in interconnected growth. Thematic ESG funds signal a commitment to sustainability; dividend aristocrats ETFs reflect a preference for established, profit-sharing businesses. In other words, ETFs allow investors to place principled bets, not on a single company's trajectory, but on broader hypotheses about the economy, society, and the future.

Yet many treat these instruments with less scrutiny than a single quarterly report. The paradox is clear: the more elegant and powerful the tool, the less it is understood. But understanding is accessible to those willing to ask the right questions.

Intentionality underpins this understanding. Every portfolio tells a story. The question is whether that story is coherent, or simply a haphazard collage of market noise and emotional reactions. Here, boredom becomes a virtue. In investing, dullness is often an indicator of health. The most resilient portfolios are rarely dramatic—they compound quietly, shielded from the market's theatrical swings. Low-cost, diversified ETFs achieve success not through spectacle, but through the cumulative avoidance of friction: fees, taxes, transaction costs, and behavioural errors.

Psychology complicates this reality. Humans crave narrative, novelty, and action. A portfolio that quietly appreciates over years may feel stagnant, prompting abandonment, while a speculative bet that plummets remains vivid because it had drama. The discipline to adhere to a slow, invisible, proven strategy is not trivial. It is, in essence, wisdom: the ability to resist the lure of excitement in favour of what is sustainable and scalable.

Ownership carries an ethical dimension often overlooked. Capital is never morally neutral. Every investment fuels enterprise, innovation, and influence—social, ecological, and political. Passive investing does not absolve responsibility; it merely shifts it to index constructors. Investors still choose which indices to follow and which sectors or practices to exclude. Aligning investment with values is not puritanical—it is recognition that money is energy directed, capable of shaping systems. ESG-focused ETFs offer a means to harmonise conscience with capital allocation, preserving diversification and efficiency while honouring principles.

This chapter reframes ownership as a philosophical stance rather than a transactional act. Investing is not a game to be won; it is a craft to be refined. Wealth is not mere accumulation—it is alignment. ETFs are not static products; they are dynamic structures reflecting beliefs about risk, value, and the future.

We will begin by interrogating the myth of foresight, illustrating why even the most skilled stock-pickers are humbled repeatedly. We will explore ETFs as composable systems encoding macroeconomic perspectives, sectoral trends, and social priorities. We will celebrate simplicity in a field addicted to complexity, and argue that strategic boredom is an asset. Finally, we will examine the moral consequences of investment choices, demonstrating that passive portfolios are not devoid of ethical impact.

These sections do not offer definitive answers; they sharpen questions. They invite you to see your portfolio not as a spreadsheet of symbols, but as a reflection of assumptions about risk, value, and the world. Ownership begins with awareness. Architecture follows.

The Myth of the Market Whisperer

There is a persistent fantasy that haunts the modern investor: the belief that somewhere, someone has cracked the code. A brilliant analyst, a bold hedge fund manager, a well-informed amateur on an investing forum—each held up as a market whisperer, someone who can see patterns others miss, someone who knows when to buy just before prices rise, and sell just before they fall. This fantasy is not merely seductive; it is foundational to much of the investing culture that surrounds us. Yet, like most myths, it thrives not because it is true, but because it offers psychological comfort in a world that is far more complex, uncertain, and uncontrollable than we wish to admit.

At the centre of this myth is the conviction that the market can be consistently outmanoeuvred by those with sufficient intelligence, research, or instinct. That the right strategy—or more commonly, the right person—can unlock above-average returns through superior foresight. The reality, however, is far less flattering to the ego. Decades of empirical data reveal a sobering pattern: the overwhelming majority of professional investors fail to outperform their benchmarks over time. And among the few who do, even fewer sustain that outperformance across multiple periods or market conditions.

A 2022 report by S&P Dow Jones Indices tracking the performance of actively managed funds found that, over a ten-year period, more than 85% of large-cap fund managers underperformed the S&P 500. This is not a recent anomaly. The pattern holds across decades, asset classes, and geographies. Even institutions armed with PhDs, powerful algorithms, and privileged information struggle to beat the brute force of the market's aggregate pricing power. If professionals cannot reliably "win," what does that say about the individual investor trading stocks between Zoom calls and podcasts?

The problem is not a lack of intellect or dedication. It is structural. Markets incorporate the collective expectations of millions of participants, each trying to price in future events faster than the next. Information, once scarce and valuable, is now ubiquitous and instantly disseminated. Competitive advantage evaporates almost as soon as it emerges. To consistently outguess this system is not just improbable—it borders on delusional.

And yet, many persist. Not because they've been misled by data, but because they've been led by psychology. The myth of the market whisperer is not primarily a failure of logic; it is a triumph of cognitive bias. We are wired to seek patterns, to overvalue recent successes, and to attribute skill where chance may be the real author. A novice investor who doubles their money on a speculative trade is not likely to credit luck. They will often believe they have a knack—an intuition. That belief fuels further risk-taking, often with disastrous results. The brain's reward circuitry mistakes randomness for reinforcement, and a temporary high becomes the prelude to a long-term mistake.

Behavioural finance has given us names for these mental missteps: overconfidence bias, confirmation bias, hindsight bias, survivorship bias. Each serves as a small nudge away from reason and toward illusion. The investor begins to see their portfolio not as a mechanism of long-term wealth building, but as a scoreboard of personal genius. Every uptick confirms their narrative; every downturn is an aberration soon to be corrected. This cognitive drift is not a symptom of ignorance—it can affect Nobel laureates as easily as novices. Intelligence, ironically, does not inoculate against these errors. In some cases, it reinforces them.

The cultural reinforcement of stock picking does not help. Financial media thrives on drama. Quiet, disciplined investing does not generate clicks. But a headline proclaiming "10 Stocks Set to Explode This Summer" is irresistible. Market commentary often treats short-term movements as meaningful, when they are frequently statistical noise. Analysts revise their outlooks daily, not because the fundamentals have changed, but because the narrative must keep moving. In this theatre of prediction, the whisperer is king—even if his crown is made of tinsel.

Against this backdrop, it becomes easy to see why passive, rules-based investing feels unsatisfying to many. There is no story. No hero. No feeling of personal brilliance. Yet paradoxically, it is this very humility—this willingness to forgo the fantasy of prediction—that often leads to better outcomes. ETFs, especially those tracking broad indices, do not promise cleverness. They promise consistency. They are not vehicles of ego, but of design. They do not require one to outguess the market, only to participate in it—patiently, systematically, and inexpensively.

Consider the case of Renaissance Technologies' Medallion Fund, one of the most successful hedge funds in history. With annualised returns north of 60% before fees, it seems to validate the dream of the market whisperer. Yet the fund is famously closed to outside investors, run by mathematicians using proprietary algorithms and high-frequency trading infrastructure inaccessible to the average person. It is the exception that proves the rule. For everyone else, chasing alpha through individual picks often amounts to little more than professionalised gambling, where luck masquerades as insight until it doesn't.

The illusion of control is perhaps the most dangerous component of this myth. Investors believe they are steering the ship when, in reality, they are often reacting to forces far beyond their comprehension. A trade may be based on diligent research, but its outcome is still subject to exogenous shocks—interest rate changes, geopolitical upheaval, supply chain disruptions, or investor sentiment swings. Control, in most investing contexts, is not achieved through precision, but through design: asset allocation, cost minimisation, risk diversification, and behavioural discipline.

One could argue that trying to beat the market is not just a poor strategy, but a misallocation of intellectual energy. The same mental bandwidth that goes into researching stock picks, timing entries, and reading technical charts could be redirected toward building a sustainable plan, understanding personal risk tolerance, or aligning investments with long-term goals. Yet the appeal of the whisperer's path remains strong because it flatters the ego. To construct a minimalist, low-cost ETF portfolio feels pedestrian—until one sees the compounding impact of such a strategy over decades.

A thought experiment is useful here. Imagine you are offered a bet: flip a coin that lands heads 60% of the time. Would you take it? Of course—over many flips, this edge virtually guarantees success. Yet many investors forgo this advantage (which broadly reflects the long-term return bias of equity markets) in favour of bets with worse odds but more narrative excitement. Stock picking feels active, ETF investing feels passive. But that language misleads. ETF investing is *not* passive—it is premeditated. It is choosing a system over a story, a process over a play.

There is also an ethical dimension rarely discussed. The myth of the market whisperer implies not only superiority, but exclusivity. If someone can reliably outperform, someone else must underperform. It is a zero-sum mindset embedded in a system that, at its best, is positive-sum. Investing through ETFs allows one to participate in the broad uplift of economies and innovation. It removes the adversarial premise and replaces it with a collaborative one: wealth is built not through vanquishing others, but through ownership in shared growth.

This section of the book does not argue that no one should ever buy individual stocks. There are cases—founder-operators, domain experts, or long-term conviction holders—where direct ownership may align with a clear and consistent thesis. But such cases are rare, and rarer still is the ability to execute them without behavioural sabotage. The average investor, no matter how intelligent, is better served by systems that remove decision-making friction, not amplify it.

To let go of the myth of the market whisperer is not to surrender. It is to mature. It is to recognise that the market does not owe us returns for cleverness, only for participation. It is to shift from trying to *win* investing to trying to *understand* it. And in that understanding, to craft a portfolio that is not a reflection of our whims, but of our values, priorities, and design.

The market does not whisper. It does not choose favourites. It rewards discipline, punishes overreach, and humbles arrogance with mechanical regularity. To stop chasing its secrets is not to give up—it is to finally begin.

From Symbols to Systems

Most investors think they are buying exposure to a set of companies when they purchase an ETF. They see a ticker symbol, perhaps glance at the top ten holdings, and assume they are acquiring a passive slice of the market—a bundle of equities conveniently wrapped in a single, tradeable unit. This perception, while not entirely wrong, is dangerously incomplete. It treats ETFs as mere containers, rather than what they truly are: engineered systems. And systems, unlike symbols, carry structure, assumptions, and embedded logic. To understand ETFs is not just to know *what* you are buying, but *how* and *why* the components are selected, weighted, and maintained. The difference is not semantic. It is foundational to making intentional, intelligent investment decisions.

ETFs do not simply *hold* assets. They *encode* investment theses. A market-cap-weighted ETF tracking the FTSE 100 expresses the idea that the largest companies in the UK economy deserve the most capital. A Nasdaq-100 tracker tilts toward growth and innovation, particularly in technology, reflecting an implicit bet on digital acceleration. A global ex-US ETF conveys a conviction—whether acknowledged or not—that opportunity lies beyond domestic borders. These are not neutral positions. They are coded beliefs, operationalised through design.

The reason this matters is because most investors treat ETFs as though they are unmediated representations of markets, as if they simply "mirror" the economy. But mirrors do not have criteria. Indices do. Every ETF is built upon a methodology—rules for inclusion, rebalancing, weighting, and turnover. These rules, often buried in technical documentation, shape outcomes in subtle but significant ways. The investor who owns an ETF owns not just a basket of securities, but a set of decisions made by index committees and product designers. When those decisions go unexamined, the investor becomes a passenger rather than a participant.

Consider the case of two ETFs both claiming to track "emerging markets." On the surface, they may appear nearly identical—similar tickers, comparable regions, shared marketing language. But a closer inspection reveals diverging methodologies. One might include South Korea as an emerging market; another might classify it as developed. One may cap exposure to China to avoid concentration risk; another may embrace it. The result is two portfolios with different country weights, risk profiles, and performance outcomes—all under the same label. The problem is not that one is superior to the other, but that many investors have no idea which system they've bought into. They see the symbol, not the structure.

This becomes even more important as ETFs evolve beyond plain-vanilla index trackers. Thematic ETFs, which bundle companies around narratives like clean energy, artificial intelligence, or blockchain innovation, do not simply represent sectors—they construct arguments. A clean energy ETF might exclude large nuclear firms despite their low emissions due to ESG screeners. An AI-focused fund might include companies that barely derive revenue from AI but score highly on "AI mentions" in earnings calls. These are not passive constructions. They are selective interpretations of complex themes, translated into investable form. If one is to invest meaningfully, these choices must be interrogated, not assumed.

There is also the issue of weighting. Most traditional ETFs use market capitalisation to allocate exposure, meaning that larger companies carry more influence. This is not a law of nature—it is a design choice. It privileges size over value, momentum over balance. It means that when you invest in a broad index, you are giving disproportionate weight to the market darlings of the moment—regardless of their fundamentals. Alternative weighting schemes exist: equal weighting, fundamental indexing, volatility-adjusted models. Each presents trade-offs in terms of turnover, cost, and performance consistency. None are inherently correct. But all demand awareness.

Understanding ETFs as systems also requires recognising the feedback loops they create. As passive investing has grown—from niche innovation in the 1990s to dominant force today—its influence on markets has become structural. Large ETF flows can amplify trends, suppress volatility, and distort price discovery in certain sectors. This is particularly true for smaller-cap or thinly traded companies that are heavily represented in popular indices. While ETFs are built to track markets, they increasingly shape them. The system becomes recursive, and passive ownership becomes a form of silent governance.

At a deeper level, ETFs allow investors to abstract away from individual companies and engage with macro ideas. A consumer staples ETF represents a belief in consistent demand across economic cycles. A frontier markets ETF signals a willingness to take geopolitical risk in exchange for potential growth. A healthcare innovation fund captures the idea that demographic shifts and technological advances will generate outsized returns. These are not "bets" in the speculative sense. They are structured expressions of belief. And when constructed carefully, they allow for a portfolio that is not only diversified by geography or sector, but by *thesis*.

Yet abstraction is a double-edged sword. It enables scale and accessibility, but can also lead to detachment. Investors may own dozens of ETFs spanning continents and industries without understanding what any of them truly represent. They may unknowingly double up on exposures, or hold contradictory positions—like simultaneously investing in ESG leaders and fossil fuel producers. This is not diversification. It is portfolio incoherence dressed up as sophistication. The solution is not to simplify for its own sake, but to reintroduce intentionality. *Every fund should earn its place.* And to earn its place, its system must be understood.

There is an ethical consideration here as well. ETFs make it easy to own the world—but they also make it easy to abdicate responsibility. When you invest in an ETF that tracks a market, you are funding the companies within it. If that market includes firms with questionable labour practices, environmental harms, or governance issues, your capital is still complicit—even if passively allocated. The system does not absolve the investor. It simply anonymises the impact. More conscientious ETFs attempt to filter for these concerns, using ESG criteria or custom exclusion screens. But even these systems are not immune to bias, opacity, or inconsistency. ESG ratings can vary wildly across providers. Inclusion criteria are rarely transparent. The investor who cares about alignment must engage critically with these systems, not just adopt their labels.

Seen through this lens, ETF investing is not about avoiding complexity—it is about *designing through* it. The simplicity on the surface masks a deep architecture of decisions, assumptions, and compromises. But this architecture can be harnessed. ETFs offer tools for modular construction, allowing investors to build portfolios that are not only diversified and low-cost, but *coherent.* A portfolio, after all, is not just a financial artefact. It is a declaration of belief: about markets, risk, opportunity, and the future.

This is what it means to move from symbols to systems. It is a shift from viewing ETFs as products to seeing them as platforms. From using them reactively to wielding them intentionally. From being a collector of funds to becoming an architect of strategy.

To invest well in ETFs is not simply to choose low fees or high returns. It is to engage with their design. To understand what they encode, whom they serve, and how they evolve. It is to move beyond surface-level identifiers and into the structural DNA of the instruments themselves.

ETFs are tools of unprecedented power and accessibility. But like all tools, their value depends on how they are understood—and how they are used. Investors who learn to see them as systems, not symbols, position themselves not just for better outcomes, but for deeper clarity. And in a financial world where opacity is too often the default, that clarity is perhaps the greatest return of all.

Why Boring Is Beautiful

Investing, for all its mathematics and mechanics, is largely a psychological endeavour. The difference between a good investor and a great one is rarely a matter of knowledge—it is almost always a matter of temperament. And yet, modern investing culture relentlessly promotes the idea that brilliance, novelty, and tactical flair are the engines of success. Complexity is sold as sophistication; volatility as opportunity. The reality, supported by decades of data and behavioural evidence, is that *boring portfolios built on low-cost, diversified ETFs tend to outperform the vast majority of flashy, high-turnover strategies—especially over the long term.* But this truth is often drowned out, not because it lacks empirical support, but because it lacks drama.

The financial industry rarely celebrates stillness. Magazines do not profile investors who quietly held a total market ETF for thirty years and retired comfortably. There are no headlines for "Investor Does Nothing and Still Beats 90% of Active Funds." The entire ecosystem—media, platforms, brokerages, influencers—depends on movement. Trades generate fees. Novelty drives clicks. The calm investor is invisible in a culture obsessed with the next big thing. But invisibility is not ineffectiveness. Some of the most successful portfolios are precisely those that appear uneventful—steady, repeatable, and utterly unremarkable in the short run, but exceptional over decades.

Consider the historical performance of broad index-tracking ETFs, such as those based on the S&P 500, the MSCI World, or total market indices. These funds are designed to be dull by nature: diversified, cap-weighted, and rebalanced to reflect market composition without attempting to outguess it. And yet, they have consistently outperformed the majority of actively managed mutual funds and hedge funds over long horizons. According to SPIVA (S&P Indices Versus Active), over a 20-year period, more than 90% of US large-cap fund managers failed to beat their benchmark after fees. The difference wasn't just cost—it was discipline. Index funds didn't try to outsmart the market; they simply stayed invested in it.

The beauty of a boring portfolio is that it avoids self-inflicted wounds. Flashy strategies often promise asymmetric upside but tend to deliver asymmetrically high risk. Tactical allocation, market timing, concentrated stock picks—all introduce decision points that invite human error. And investors, even professional ones, are astonishingly bad at making high-stakes decisions under emotional pressure. Behavioural finance has repeatedly demonstrated that the average investor underperforms the very funds they invest in, simply because they mistime their entries and exits—buying after euphoria, selling during panic. A dull portfolio sidesteps this trap by design. It reduces optionality, not through limitation, but through intentionality.

There is, of course, an emotional cost to this kind of discipline. Boring is not only unglamorous—it is often *uncomfortable.* In a rising market, the ETF investor watches friends brag about triple-digit returns on speculative assets. In a falling market, they resist the temptation to sell "before it gets worse." They endure periods where their portfolio lags the market's latest darling—tech one year, energy the next, cryptocurrency the year after. They commit to a long-term thesis that doesn't always feel good in the short term. And yet, *it is precisely this discomfort that makes long-term outperformance possible.* Because boring portfolios do not chase. They compound.

There is a useful analogy in agriculture. A farmer does not constantly dig up crops to check if they are growing. The work is in the planting, not the constant meddling. Similarly, the returns of a long-term ETF portfolio are rarely a function of quarterly brilliance. They are the result of consistency, cost control, and the relentless march of compound returns over time. But like farming, investing with patience requires trust in a process that offers little immediate feedback. That trust is often eroded by a financial culture that rewards action and ridicules inertia.

The psychological difficulty of doing nothing should not be underestimated. It requires a different kind of intelligence—not the ability to identify obscure signals, but the ability to ignore noise. To filter out the daily fluctuations, the macro commentary, the economic forecasts, and the endless stream of content designed to provoke action. A low-cost ETF portfolio, rebalanced periodically, seems insultingly simple to many investors. It feels like an under-reaction to a complex world. But simplicity is not the same as naïveté. In investing, simplicity often represents the highest form of sophistication—*a clarity that emerges only after confronting and rejecting the illusions of control.*

Flashy strategies appeal because they suggest agency. The idea that one can respond to volatility with tactical brilliance is emotionally satisfying. It offers the illusion that markets are problems to be solved rather than environments to be endured. But volatility is not a glitch—it is a feature. Over any long-term investment horizon, downturns are inevitable, drawdowns are routine, and corrections are common. The question is not whether you can avoid them, but whether you can stay invested through them. Flashy strategies promise escape; boring portfolios provide resilience.

There are also structural advantages to boring. A portfolio built on ETFs tends to have lower turnover, which means lower transaction costs and fewer taxable events. This is not trivial. Taxes, like fees, are silent performance killers. Every unnecessary trade may come with an embedded cost that erodes returns quietly but relentlessly. The compounding effect of minimising these frictions over decades is enormous. It is not flashy, but it is real. And it is measurable.

It's worth noting that boring does not mean static. A well-constructed ETF portfolio can evolve. It can be tilted toward different factors—value, momentum, dividends. It can incorporate global exposure, thematic elements, or ethical considerations. But these changes are strategic, not reactive. They are implemented as part of a broader design, not in response to headlines. The key distinction is *intention.* A boring portfolio may be dynamic in structure but stable in philosophy. It does not chase outcomes—it builds for them.

There is, of course, a counterargument: that risk-taking and innovation are rewarded in markets, and that active strategies, when executed well, can outperform. This is true in isolated cases. There are managers who beat benchmarks, investors who spot trends early, and tactical allocations that deliver outperformance. But these are the exceptions, not the rule—and the difficulty lies not in identifying them after the fact, but in *choosing them in advance and sticking with them through underperformance.* The average investor, when presented with a long list of active funds or clever strategies, tends to select the one that recently outperformed—only to abandon it once mean reversion sets in. The problem is not ambition; it is execution.

Boring portfolios, by contrast, make fewer promises but deliver more consistently. They don't attempt to optimise every variable. They aim for sufficiency over perfection, stability over spectacle. And in doing so, they create the psychological conditions necessary for investors to stay invested. Because *the best strategy is not the one with the highest theoretical return—it is the one you can actually follow.* A portfolio that produces 8% annualised returns over 30 years, held through all market cycles, will almost always outperform a 12% strategy that is abandoned during downturns.

What's more, boring portfolios free up mental bandwidth. Investors who aren't constantly analysing markets, second-guessing trades, or chasing trends can devote their attention to more important questions: Are my investments aligned with my goals? Am I funding the future I actually want? Do my spending and saving habits match my values? This shift—from performance to purpose—is one of the most powerful transformations an investor can undergo. And it begins by relinquishing the need for excitement in favour of clarity.

The cultural resistance to boring strategies stems from a deep misunderstanding of what investing is supposed to accomplish. It is not meant to be entertaining. It is meant to be effective. It is not meant to reflect brilliance; it is meant to reflect commitment. The most important decisions in investing are not what to buy or when to sell, but whether you are willing to embrace a process that works quietly, even when no one is watching.

To call an ETF portfolio "boring" is not a criticism—it is a compliment. It means the portfolio is doing exactly what it was designed to do: provide exposure, minimise cost, reduce behavioural errors, and deliver market returns over time. In a world where noise is mistaken for signal and activity for progress, the ability to remain boring is not a weakness—it is a rare form of strength. And for those who can embrace it, the rewards are not just financial, but philosophical: a sense of calm in a culture of chaos, a system that works when you don't, and the quiet satisfaction of knowing that boring, properly executed, is often the most beautiful strategy of all.

Investing as a Moral Act

Every pound you invest is a form of power. It may not feel like it. Investing, especially in ETFs, is often framed as passive—a mechanical, apolitical act. You buy exposure to a market, track an index, and let compounding do the rest. But behind the tickers and allocations, real companies receive your capital. They use it to expand operations, develop products, lobby governments, and influence societies. To invest, even passively, is to participate in shaping the world. The idea that investing is neutral—merely a tool for building personal wealth without consequence—is no longer tenable. If your money is at work, then so, too, is your influence. And like any influence, it has moral weight.

Modern investing has been structured, almost by design, to obscure this reality. Markets are intermediated by platforms, fund providers, and financial products that distance the investor from the enterprise. When you invest in an ETF, you may hold fractional shares in hundreds or thousands of companies, many of which you will never research, never interact with, and possibly never even recognise. This abstraction is efficient but not ethically empty. It creates a form of plausible deniability: "I didn't choose to fund oil companies or surveillance firms—my ETF did." Yet the outcome is the same. Capital is allocated, dividends flow, share prices rise, and executives are empowered. Responsibility, while diffused, is not erased.

The notion that investing carries ethical implications is not new, but it is only recently that this awareness has begun to influence mainstream portfolio construction. Environmental, Social and Governance (ESG) frameworks, once considered niche, have become central to the investment strategies of major institutions and increasingly accessible to individual investors. But ESG itself is not a moral compass—it is a set of criteria, inconsistently applied, sometimes opaque, and often shaped by competing incentives. What matters is not the presence of an ESG label, but the clarity of the investor's own values and the rigour with which they align their portfolio to them.

This is where ETFs offer both a challenge and an opportunity. The challenge lies in the fact that most ETFs, particularly broad-market trackers, are designed for scale and liquidity—not moral discernment. They include whatever the underlying index dictates. If the S&P 500 includes weapons manufacturers or companies with controversial labour practices, so does the ETF. There is no ethical screening, because that is not the function of the index. Yet this lack of screening is itself a choice—a decision to prioritise comprehensiveness over conscience. The question becomes: is that acceptable to you?

Some investors will say yes, viewing the market as a neutral playing field and preferring to keep personal values and financial strategy separate. But increasingly, others are asking harder questions. If my portfolio contributes to climate change, do the returns still feel like success? If I profit from supply chains that exploit workers, am I complicit? These are not easy questions, nor do they admit simple answers. But avoiding them entirely is not neutrality—it is abdication.

Fortunately, the ETF universe has expanded to offer more tools for ethically engaged investors. There are now funds that screen for carbon emissions, that exclude controversial weapons, that tilt toward companies with strong governance or positive social impact. These are imperfect solutions, subject to limitations and inconsistencies. But they represent an important shift: from a passive view of investing as ownership without agency, to a more conscious model in which capital allocation is treated as a form of stewardship.

It is also worth acknowledging that ethical investing does not always mean sacrificing returns. Numerous studies suggest that companies with robust ESG practices may be more resilient, more innovative, and better governed. These traits can translate into competitive advantages and, ultimately, into long-term performance. But even if that weren't the case, the more fundamental argument remains: *alignment with values is itself a form of return.* A portfolio that reflects your convictions—not just your financial goals, but your principles—offers a kind of coherence that transcends yield.

This is especially relevant for long-term investors. Over decades, the companies you invest in will have profound effects on society—on the environment, on employment, on the direction of technology and culture. A passive ETF investor might see themselves as disconnected from these forces, but the cumulative impact of billions of such "disconnected" decisions is precisely what drives systemic outcomes. If we treat the market as a machine that operates without moral consequence, we shouldn't be surprised when its outputs become misaligned with human values.

There is a deeper tension here worth exploring. Many people invest for personal security—for retirement, education, freedom. These are legitimate, even noble aims. But what if the means of achieving that security contribute to instability elsewhere? What if the profits that fund your child's education come from the emissions that degrade another's future? Ethical investing does not require perfection, but it *does* require reflection. It invites you to consider the trade-offs, to examine the stories behind the returns, and to accept that your investments are not just statements about risk and reward—but about who you are and what you stand for.

This also reframes the role of financial literacy. To be financially literate in the 21st century is not just to understand diversification, fees, and compound interest. It is to understand how capital flows affect real-world systems. It is to question how your brokerage account interacts with supply chains, environmental policy, labour standards, and innovation. Passive investing, once seen as the most hands-off approach, now demands a more active form of ethical awareness. You may not pick stocks—but you *do* pick systems.

Some will argue that the impact of individual investors is too small to matter. That unless institutional capital moves, little will change. This is a misunderstanding of both market mechanics and collective agency. ETFs are built on aggregate flows. Index constructors adjust constituents based on criteria and demand. Fund providers respond to investor preferences. Change, in markets as in democracy, is often driven by pressure at the margins. When enough individuals act intentionally, the system evolves.

To be clear, this is not a call for moral absolutism. The world is complex, and markets reflect that complexity. Every company has flaws; every fund is an imperfect proxy. Ethical investing is not about purity—it is about *effort.* It is about choosing coherence over convenience, asking uncomfortable questions, and building portfolios that not only fund your future, but also your integrity. It is not always easy. But ease was never the point. *Meaning rarely is.*

Ultimately, investing is not just a financial decision—it is a philosophical one. It reflects how you see the world, what you believe about human progress, and where you want to place your trust. If you believe that capitalism can be a force for good, then your investments should reflect that belief. If you believe that certain industries harm more than they help, your capital can be withheld. ETFs, far from being blunt instruments, can be refined into tools of ethical expression. But only if the investor brings intention to the table.

There is a profound difference between investing for a return and investing for a legacy. The former asks, "What can I get?" The latter asks, "What am I building?" Your portfolio is part of that answer. Not just a collection of assets, but a reflection of values. Not just a financial plan, but a moral stance. To invest with clarity is to own not just the shares, but the consequences. And that is where the real power—and responsibility—of investing begins.

Chapter 2
The ETF: An Elegant Machine

It is a curious paradox of contemporary investing that one of its most transformative innovations remains among the least understood. The exchange-traded fund, or ETF, has become so ubiquitous—so easily accessible, so superficially simple—that most investors engage with it without pausing to grasp its inner workings. Purchased with a few taps, slotted into portfolios with minimal fanfare, ETFs appear almost banal. Yet behind the unassuming ticker lies an engineering feat: a finely tuned mechanism that has quietly reshaped global capital allocation.

To call an ETF merely a "basket of stocks" is convenient shorthand, but it obscures the deeper reality. ETFs are intentionally designed instruments, governed by legal frameworks, market mechanics, and algorithmic discipline. They merge the accessibility of equities with the diversification of mutual funds while eliminating many inefficiencies inherent in both. Their brilliance lies not merely in the assets they hold, but in how they hold them—and in the manner they grant investors access to complex markets with efficiency, transparency, and control.

This chapter treats the ETF not as a product, but as a system. Like all powerful tools, it warrants examination—its architecture, evolution, and the mechanisms driving performance. Intelligent use of ETFs requires understanding their structural underpinnings: what ensures liquidity, what keeps costs low, and how design fosters disciplined behaviour in ways traditional vehicles often cannot. This is knowledge not for its own sake, but as the foundation of confident, deliberate investing.

We begin with structure. An ETF blends fund and stock: a pooled vehicle traded like a single security on an exchange. Beneath the surface, however, the operation is intricate. Creation and redemption processes, in-kind transfers, and arbitrage mechanisms—these are the gears and pulleys that keep an ETF's price aligned with net asset value, while maintaining liquidity and tax efficiency. Unlike mutual funds, which price at day's end and require purchases through the provider, ETFs are continuously priced, supported by authorised participants and market makers who smooth trading, even amid volatility.

This design was intentional, forged through decades of refinement. The SPDR S&P 500 ETF Trust, launched in 1993, allowed investors to buy the entire market in one trade—a concept rooted in earlier academic debates on index investing, regulatory innovation, and real-time pricing technology. From a niche experiment, ETFs have become central to global finance. Today, they manage over US$10 trillion, spanning retirement accounts to institutional hedging. They are no longer peripheral; they are foundational.

Yet ubiquity breeds complacency. Many investors overlook the mechanisms that confer efficiency. Index tracking, for instance, is more than allocation—it is automation. It removes discretionary decision-making, reduces costs, minimises turnover, and shields investors from emotion. But automation carries questions: how is the index constructed, who decides inclusions, and how are rule changes managed? Understanding methodology is essential for purposeful investment.

Rebalancing illustrates another structural advantage. Traditional portfolios require manual, often neglected adjustments; ETFs tied to indices rebalance automatically according to provider schedules. This mechanical process enforces discipline: trimming winners, topping up losers, and maintaining intended exposures. Over time, it compounds behavioural benefits, embedding systematic, emotion-free portfolio maintenance—a feat many investors struggle to achieve independently.

Cost is equally significant. Beyond headline expense ratios, ETFs offer lower trading costs, minimal capital gains distributions through in-kind transfers, and the flexibility to adjust exposure without restructuring portfolios. Even small differences, like a 0.1% expense ratio, compound over decades, underscoring the importance of friction minimisation. Carefully chosen ETFs offer a path to long-term wealth with remarkably low drag.

Yet efficiency is not neutrality. The very traits that make ETFs appealing—simplicity, automation, low cost—can mask complexity. Two ETFs tracking the same index may differ in replication method, issuer quality, or tracking error. Thoughtful investors scrutinise these structural nuances, recognising that choices such as synthetic versus physical replication or full versus optimised sampling can materially affect performance, tax treatment, and risk.

Philosophically, ETFs represent a shift from individual security selection to systemic participation. They reflect a worldview: that markets reward broad engagement more consistently than selective prediction. Design substitutes for insight; consistency outperforms conviction. But without comprehension, the ETF risks being treated as a convenient instrument rather than a deliberate tool.

In the following pages, we explore the ETF as a mechanism: its components, processes, and safeguards; its history from experimental product to global standard; the hidden levers that enable performance—indexing, rebalancing, arbitrage; and the costs of inattention. Discipline, more than timing or talent, emerges as the decisive factor in long-term success.

The ETF is not magical. It guarantees nothing. Yet its elegance—simple in form, powerful in function, precise in achieving its objectives—is undeniable. To invest through ETFs is to engage with one of the most refined financial innovations of the past half-century. Effective use requires understanding not merely what an ETF is, but what it enables: deliberate, efficient, and disciplined wealth construction. This chapter is an invitation into that comprehension, blending technical, historical, and philosophical insight into a tool that quietly transforms modern investing.

Anatomy of an ETF

To understand why exchange-traded funds (ETFs) have reshaped the investment landscape, one must first look past their surface simplicity. They trade like a stock, track like a fund, and cost less than either active management or direct equity diversification. But these qualities are outcomes of a deeper engineering—of structural decisions, market mechanisms, and legal frameworks that make the ETF not only accessible, but *elegant.* It is precisely this design—deliberate, resilient, and quietly sophisticated—that gives ETFs their unique position in modern finance. To invest through them wisely requires fluency in how they work, not just what they hold.

At their core, ETFs are pooled investment vehicles, much like mutual funds. They collect capital from investors and use that capital to buy a portfolio of underlying securities—typically equities, bonds, commodities, or a mixture thereof. But the similarity ends there. What distinguishes ETFs from traditional funds is how they're *built*, how they *trade*, and how they're *maintained.* Each of these domains contributes to their low cost, high transparency, and operational liquidity—features that, when understood, can significantly improve the quality of an investor's decisions.

Start with structure. ETFs are typically organised as open-ended investment companies or unit trusts, depending on jurisdiction, and are governed by a prospectus that outlines their objective, underlying index (if passive), and operational guidelines. Unlike closed-end funds, which issue a fixed number of shares and often trade at a premium or discount to net asset value (NAV), ETFs rely on a unique mechanism known as *creation and redemption in kind.* This system—often overlooked by end investors—is the bedrock of the ETF's functional integrity.

Here's how it works. Instead of buying and selling shares directly with retail investors, ETF providers interact with a group of institutional intermediaries known as *authorised participants* (APs). These APs have the right to create or redeem ETF shares in large blocks, often referred to as *creation units.* When demand for an ETF rises, an AP assembles a basket of the underlying securities that mirrors the ETF's index and delivers it to the fund issuer. In exchange, they receive newly created ETF shares, which they can then sell on the open market. Conversely, when redemptions occur, the AP returns ETF shares to the provider and receives the equivalent basket of underlying securities.

This process is conducted *in-kind*, meaning securities are exchanged directly rather than settled in cash. This has two powerful advantages: it minimises capital gains distributions (because the fund is not liquidating assets), and it facilitates a natural arbitrage process that keeps the ETF's market price tightly aligned with its NAV. If the ETF trades above NAV, APs can profit by delivering the underlying securities and selling the ETF shares for more; if it trades below, they can do the reverse. This built-in mechanism ensures that price deviations are typically small and short-lived—*a market-based self-correction system that protects the end investor without requiring intervention.*

Trading is another area where ETFs break with tradition. Mutual funds can only be bought or sold at the end-of-day NAV, once the fund has calculated the value of its holdings. ETFs, by contrast, trade continuously throughout the day like stocks. This intraday liquidity offers flexibility: investors can buy on dips, set limit orders, and hedge positions in real time. It also opens the door to tighter spreads, more precise price discovery, and the ability to implement tactical shifts without waiting for the bell. But it also introduces risks—particularly for less liquid ETFs or those tracking volatile or complex assets. Bid-ask spreads can widen under stress, and investors unaware of how underlying asset liquidity affects ETF pricing may find themselves on the wrong side of a trade. *Liquidity, in ETFs, is not uniform—it depends on both the secondary market and the liquidity of the underlying holdings.*

Transparency is another defining feature. Most ETFs publish their full list of holdings daily—a level of disclosure far beyond what most mutual funds offer. This visibility allows investors to know exactly what they own, how the portfolio is constructed, and whether it aligns with their broader strategy. It also supports accountability. If an ESG-labelled ETF includes holdings that contradict an investor's values, that discrepancy is visible. If a sector ETF drifts into style bias or concentration, the evidence is there. This level of openness may seem mundane, but it plays a critical role in investor trust. *You cannot invest intentionally in what you cannot see clearly.*

Cost, too, is baked into the ETF's anatomy. Because most ETFs are passively managed—tracking indices rather than attempting to outperform them—they avoid the management fees, research overhead, and trading costs associated with active stock-picking. This structural cost advantage is further enhanced by the in-kind redemption system, which, as noted, mitigates taxable events. But investors should not assume all ETFs are cheap. Specialty funds, actively managed ETFs, or those with complex strategies often carry higher fees. Moreover, *trading costs, bid-ask spreads, and tracking error*—the divergence between the ETF's performance and its benchmark—must also be factored into the true cost of ownership.

And then there's the critical distinction between *physical* and *synthetic* ETFs—a subtle but important difference in replication method. Physical ETFs own the underlying securities directly. Synthetic ETFs, by contrast, use derivatives—typically total return swaps—with counterparties to replicate the performance of the index. While both aim to deliver similar returns, synthetic structures carry counterparty risk and greater complexity. In some markets, such as Europe, synthetic ETFs are more common due to regulatory and tax advantages. For informed investors, this distinction matters. Not because one is inherently better, but because each introduces different layers of exposure, transparency, and operational risk.

These design features—creation/redemption, intraday trading, transparency, low cost, and replication strategy—make ETFs a uniquely modular tool. They can be used to build core portfolios, express tactical views, gain access to niche asset classes, or implement factor tilts with surgical precision. But modularity can be a double-edged sword. It invites customisation but also over-engineering. The proliferation of ETFs—now numbering in the thousands—means investors must apply judgement, not just diversification. Two funds with similar names may differ dramatically in methodology, weighting, and rebalancing rules. *Without fluency in ETF mechanics, the risk of misalignment increases—between intention and exposure, expectation and outcome.*

The contrast with mutual funds sharpens the ETF's appeal. Mutual funds, while still dominant in many retirement accounts, suffer from limitations: lack of intraday liquidity, opaque pricing, frequent capital gains distributions, and higher costs. Their closed architecture places control in the hands of the fund manager and requires trust in discretion. ETFs shift the locus of control back to the investor—providing autonomy, visibility, and efficiency. This shift is not merely cosmetic; it reflects a broader transformation in how capital markets now operate. Investors are no longer passive recipients of performance. With ETFs, they become allocators of exposure, engineers of strategy, and managers of their own behavioural risk.

But understanding structure is not an endpoint—it is a foundation. Knowing how ETFs work gives investors the ability to ask better questions: *Is this fund appropriate for my objective? Do I understand how it behaves in volatile markets? What are the trade-offs between cost, precision, and complexity?* Fluency in the anatomy of an ETF transforms an investor from a consumer of financial products into a discerning user of financial systems.

Ultimately, ETFs are not about hype—they are about access. Access to markets, to strategies, to ideas once reserved for institutions. But access without comprehension can be dangerous. To benefit fully from what ETFs offer, one must look past the surface simplicity and engage with the mechanism. Only then does the ETF reveal itself—not just as a convenient wrapper for returns, but as an elegantly constructed tool for building financial futures with intention and insight.

The Birth of a Financial Innovation

It is easy to forget that the exchange-traded fund, now a cornerstone of modern investing, began as a regulatory curiosity and a product of financial discontent. Today, ETFs are central to how trillions of dollars are allocated, influencing capital flows, portfolio design, and even corporate governance. But their origins were neither inevitable nor universally welcomed. The ETF's rise from obscure innovation to financial infrastructure reflects a larger transformation in how we think about ownership, efficiency, and access to markets. To understand that ascent is to better understand the philosophy behind its design—and why it has come to dominate not just retail portfolios, but the architecture of global investing itself.

The roots of the ETF lie in the intellectual revolution around passive investing. In the 1960s and 70s, economists like Eugene Fama and Burton Malkiel advanced the notion that markets were broadly efficient—that is, prices already reflected all available information, and attempting to outguess them was statistically futile over time. The academic consensus began to tilt against the idea of consistent outperformance through stock picking. Jack Bogle's creation of the Vanguard 500 Index Fund in 1976 was the first practical manifestation of that belief—a vehicle that sought simply to mirror the market rather than outwit it. It was ridiculed at launch as "un-American," but it marked a profound shift: *investing could now be about participation, not prediction.*

Yet index funds had limitations. They were structured as mutual funds, meaning they priced only once per day, could not be traded intraday, and were often less tax-efficient than their investors realised. The next logical step was to bring the indexing philosophy to a product with the flexibility of a stock—something that could be bought and sold at will, offered real-time pricing, and allowed for more efficient creation and redemption. But this idea collided with legal, regulatory, and operational obstacles for years before anyone could make it viable.

The earliest attempt to bridge this gap came in 1989, with the launch of Index Participation Shares (IPS) by the American Stock Exchange. These were designed to track the S&P 500 and trade on an exchange. The concept was simple enough: create an investable share representing the performance of the index, allowing traders to gain exposure without buying all 500 constituent stocks. But the product was swiftly challenged by the Chicago Mercantile Exchange, which viewed IPS as a competitor to its index futures contracts. The U.S. Securities and Exchange Commission (SEC) sided with the CME, and the product was pulled from the market. The ETF almost died before it was born.

But the setback prompted innovation, not retreat. In 1990, the Toronto Stock Exchange quietly launched the Toronto 35 Index Participation Units (TIPs), a product that tracked the TSE-35 Index and allowed intraday trading. It worked. While TIPs never achieved global recognition, they provided a working prototype for what an ETF could be—a live, tradeable, index-tracking vehicle with structural efficiency. The idea had been validated.

Then, in 1993, the game changed. State Street Global Advisors, in partnership with the American Stock Exchange, launched the SPDR S&P 500 ETF (ticker: SPY). It was the first ETF in the United States to be both legally durable and commercially viable. Its structure relied on a new regulatory innovation: exemptive relief from the Investment Company Act of 1940, which allowed the ETF to operate like a mutual fund in terms of diversification and investor protection, but trade like a stock. The product was designed with a dual-market system: retail investors would trade ETF shares on the secondary market, while institutional participants would manage share creation and redemption in the primary market using in-kind transfers.

The innovation worked so well that SPY still exists today, managing over $400 billion in assets and remaining one of the most liquid securities in the world. But its success was not immediate. The ETF market took years to mature. Throughout the 1990s, issuers experimented with sector ETFs, international variants, and fixed-income exposures. The financial industry was cautious, even sceptical. Many fund managers saw ETFs as a threat to active management revenue. Advisers were unsure how to explain them to clients. And regulators remained wary of products that combined features of both equities and funds.

The real acceleration came after the dot-com crash in the early 2000s. Investors burned by speculative stock picking began looking for safer, lower-cost ways to stay exposed to the market. At the same time, the internet boom had democratised access to trading platforms and financial information. Retail investors, now more empowered than ever, began to see the appeal of vehicles that offered institutional-grade diversification at a fraction of the cost. ETFs, quietly, started to capture inflows once reserved for mutual funds.

By the time the 2008 global financial crisis arrived, ETFs had become not only viable, but necessary. In a world suddenly obsessed with transparency, liquidity, and risk control, the ETF's structural advantages became impossible to ignore. Investors could see what they owned, trade it immediately, and avoid many of the tax headaches associated with fund redemptions. In-kind creation/redemption mechanisms reduced the need for fund managers to sell assets at a loss. Index-tracking products, stripped of discretionary judgement, avoided the catastrophic underperformance that plagued many active funds during the downturn. *The ETF became a form of financial insurance—not against loss, but against opacity, cost, and misalignment.*

Since then, growth has been exponential. The ETF market has expanded from a few dozen products in the late 1990s to thousands of funds today, covering everything from global equities and fixed income to commodities, volatility strategies, thematic sectors, and leveraged bets. Asset managers like BlackRock (via iShares),

Vanguard, and State Street now manage trillions through ETFs, while new entrants continue to innovate with environmental, social, and governance (ESG) screening, direct indexing capabilities, and even actively managed ETF structures. In some cases, ETFs have grown so large that they've started to reshape the indices they track—*a recursive loop where passive investing is no longer simply a mirror of the market, but an influence on its form.*

This raises legitimate concerns. Some critics argue that ETFs concentrate market power in the hands of a few providers. Others worry that ETF flows distort price discovery, increase systemic risk, or encourage herd behaviour. While many of these fears are overstated—or rest on misinterpretations of how ETFs function—they are not without merit. Any tool that grows this influential deserves scrutiny. But what's clear is that the ETF is no longer an experiment. It is infrastructure. It sits at the heart of how pension funds allocate capital, how advisers build models, and how individuals access markets. It is no longer the alternative—it is the default.

What makes the ETF's evolution so striking is not just its speed, but the philosophical realignment it represents. The ETF embodies a shift from narrative-based investing to structure-based investing. It moves the locus of decision-making from stock selection to asset allocation, from timing trades to designing exposures. It encourages behavioural discipline through automation and systematisation. And perhaps most importantly, it redefines what it means to be a shareholder. No longer just a picker of winners, the ETF investor becomes a participant in the system itself—owning slices of markets, sectors, or themes through a vehicle that abstracts away the drama and focuses on process.

To understand the birth of the ETF is to see not just a new product, but a new philosophy. One that privileges access over exclusivity, clarity over complexity, and long-term alignment over short-term outperformance. It is the financial equivalent of moving from bespoke tailoring to engineered design: scalable, precise, and democratic. And like all great innovations, its true genius lies not in complexity, but in elegance. The ETF did not reinvent investing—it reimagined how it could be delivered. That distinction is why it has lasted, and why its influence will only continue to grow.

The Hidden Levers: Indexing and Rebalancing

The hallmark of intelligent investing is not brilliance at picking winners, but the discipline to stay aligned with a strategy that works quietly and consistently over time. In this context, two features built into well-constructed ETFs—*index tracking* and *automatic rebalancing*—are often dismissed as mere conveniences. In reality, they are among the most powerful levers available to long-term investors. Not because they offer excitement, but because they strip away noise, eliminate behavioural friction, and anchor a portfolio in principles rather than predictions. They represent the quiet architecture beneath sustained wealth-building—precise, repeatable, and remarkably resilient.

Start with index tracking. The modern ETF ecosystem is built on indices—rules-based collections of securities designed to represent specific markets, sectors, or investment themes. The job of an index-tracking ETF is not to outperform that benchmark, but to replicate it with high fidelity and low cost. This may sound underwhelming, but it reflects a foundational insight from decades of research: *most active strategies fail to beat their benchmark consistently, especially after fees*. By design, index tracking allows the investor to bypass the costly pursuit of outperformance in favour of broad, efficient market participation.

But indexing is more than mimicry. It is a form of systematised exposure. The underlying methodology of an index—how securities are selected, weighted, and rebalanced—has profound implications for return, risk, and portfolio behaviour. Consider the difference between a market-cap-weighted index, which allocates more to the largest companies, and an equal-weighted index, which spreads exposure uniformly. Both track "the market," but they behave differently in practice. Likewise, an index may include profitability filters, sector caps, or regional constraints that affect performance. These design choices encode investment philosophies—sometimes implicitly—into passive products.

That makes index literacy essential. Investors who assume all indices are equivalent risk misunderstanding what they're truly exposed to. Two ETFs tracking "global equities" can diverge significantly depending on whether they include emerging markets, how they handle currency risk, or how they weight their constituents. Indexing is not neutral. It is a codified worldview, embedded into rules. *To track an index is to adopt its assumptions.* Passive is not thoughtless. It is premeditated.

What makes indexing so powerful, though, is not merely its logic—it is its *discipline.* By outsourcing selection to a rule set, investors remove themselves from the most dangerous part of the process: decision-making under emotional pressure. When markets fall, a disciplined index strategy doesn't flinch. It doesn't ask whether now is the right time to sell or which stocks are safe. It simply rebalances according to schedule. That absence of panic is not a lack of intelligence—it is the presence of design. Indexing allows investors to sidestep not just the errors of others, but their own worst instincts.

And yet, even the best index can drift from its intended purpose without rebalancing. This is where the second hidden lever—automatic rebalancing—enters. Rebalancing is the process of realigning a portfolio to its target asset allocation, trimming positions that have grown too large and adding to those that have shrunk. In theory, this sounds simple. In practice, it requires going against emotion. Rebalancing often means selling recent winners and buying recent losers—precisely the opposite of what most investors feel inclined to do. It is, fundamentally, a contrarian act.

Most individuals do not rebalance consistently. They either forget, delay, or override the process when markets are volatile. This introduces drift, and with it, unintended risk. A portfolio that starts as 60/40 equity/bonds can easily morph into 80/20 in a rising market, amplifying exposure without conscious consent. The beauty of many index-based ETFs is that they internalise this process. When structured properly—especially in the case of balanced or multi-asset ETFs—they rebalance automatically, either periodically or based on tolerance thresholds. This feature is often marketed as convenience. It is better understood as *behavioural armour.*

Rebalancing is also a return generator, though not in the conventional sense. It does not add alpha by picking better stocks or timing sectors. It adds value by enforcing a rules-based discipline that systematically buys low and sells high—slowly, incrementally, and with remarkable consistency over time. This effect may be modest in any given year, but over decades, it can meaningfully improve risk-adjusted returns. More importantly, it keeps the investor's exposure aligned with their original intent. It safeguards the design.

One of the most elegant expressions of this can be seen in lifecycle or target-date ETFs. These products shift asset allocation automatically over time, moving from higher-growth equities in early years to more stable fixed-income instruments as the investor nears retirement. The rebalancing is pre-programmed, removing the need for tactical adjustments and emotional decision-making. While not perfect, these structures demonstrate how indexing and rebalancing, when combined intelligently, can deliver a glide path to financial goals with minimal intervention.

Critics argue that such automation introduces rigidity—that it may fail to adapt to market conditions or macroeconomic shifts. But this misses the point. The strength of index-based rebalancing is not its sensitivity to short-term conditions, but its *resilience across long-term ones.* Markets are noisy. Narratives shift. But the core drivers of long-term returns—asset allocation, costs, behavioural consistency—

remain. Automation is not a limitation. It is a design choice to prioritise signal over noise.

There are, of course, structural considerations. Not all ETFs rebalance internally. Single-asset ETFs (e.g., those tracking the S&P 500 or a sector index) require the investor to rebalance across holdings if used in a portfolio. This makes understanding the *level of the system* at which rebalancing occurs critical. A well-diversified ETF of ETFs may include internal rebalancing across asset classes. A DIY three-fund portfolio requires the investor to do it manually. Both are valid approaches, but only when implemented with consistency and awareness.

Tracking error is another subtle aspect of indexing. It measures how closely an ETF mirrors its benchmark and can result from replication methods, fees, or rebalancing lags. While small in well-constructed ETFs, tracking error can accumulate. Investors who expect perfect correlation must understand that even passive funds are subject to real-world frictions. Replication is precise, but not flawless.

At its best, the combination of indexing and rebalancing delivers a system that is self-correcting, cost-efficient, and behaviourally sustainable. It's a system that does not require forecasts, heroics, or market clairvoyance. It simply requires design—and trust in that design. The irony is that these hidden levers are often overlooked precisely because they do not demand constant attention. They are not sold with urgency. They do not promise excitement. They simply work.

And that is their genius. They transform investing from an act of performance into an act of alignment. They allow the investor to participate in the productivity of markets without constantly second-guessing their strategy. In a financial world saturated with noise, the silent, steady work of indexing and rebalancing offers something rare: *a structure that rewards patience, not prediction.* Understanding these mechanisms is not just a technical exercise—it is a shift in mindset.

It is the recognition that true control in investing comes not from reacting better, but from designing systems that require fewer reactions altogether.

Fees, Friction, and the Cost of Inattention

If compound interest is the engine of long-term wealth creation, then costs—tiny, persistent, and often hidden—are its slow, silent leak. The difference between a 6.8% and a 6.5% annual return may seem trivial on paper. Over a single year, it hardly registers. Over three decades, however, that 0.3% compounds into a material gap in final portfolio value—often tens of thousands, even hundreds of thousands, in lost capital. And yet, many investors spend far more time debating market timing or stock selection than scrutinising the cost structure of their holdings. It's not because they don't care. It's because the cost of inattention is rarely felt immediately. It accumulates invisibly, like slow erosion on a cliff face—unnoticed until the foundation gives way.

In the world of ETFs, low fees are rightly celebrated. The industry was built on the principle that investors deserve access to diversified market exposure at minimal cost. Index tracking, automation, and competition have driven expense ratios down to astonishing levels—many broad-market ETFs now charge less than 0.10%, and some have reached zero. But cost is never a single number. The headline expense ratio, while important, is only one part of the equation. Total cost of ownership also includes bid–ask spreads, tracking error, trading commissions (where applicable), slippage, tax drag, and fund structure nuances. These are often harder to quantify and easier to ignore, but together they can compound into meaningful performance decay.

Start with expense ratios, the most visible and often most misunderstood cost metric. A 0.07% annual fee on a broad market ETF seems negligible, and in relative terms, it is. But that's the point: relative comparisons matter. If one fund charges 0.07% and another

0.30% to track the same index, the second must justify its higher cost with either improved tracking precision or secondary benefits such as better liquidity or a more robust issuer. Otherwise, it's simply siphoning value. The market has grown so competitive that many higher-fee ETFs now persist not because they deliver better performance, but because of inertia—legacy allocation, brand loyalty, or adviser relationships that discourage change. *Cost, like convenience, compounds silently when left unexamined.*

Then there's bid–ask spread—the invisible toll every investor pays when buying or selling an ETF. Unlike mutual funds, which transact at NAV once per day, ETFs trade throughout the day on exchanges. The spread between what a buyer is willing to pay (bid) and what a seller demands (ask) may only be a few basis points in a liquid ETF, but that spread is a cost. For small, frequently traded funds—say, SPY or VTI—the spread is often just a penny. But for niche ETFs with low volume or exotic exposure, it can widen substantially, especially during periods of market stress. A poorly timed trade in a low-liquidity ETF can result in meaningful slippage—*not because the fund is flawed, but because the investor misunderstood its real trading cost.*

This links directly to liquidity—not just of the ETF itself, but of the underlying assets. An ETF may appear liquid based on its daily trading volume, but that volume reflects secondary market activity. The true constraint is the liquidity of the securities within the ETF. An ETF tracking U.S. large caps will generally be as liquid as the market itself. But one tracking frontier markets, high-yield bonds, or rare commodities may exhibit significant pricing friction, particularly during volatile periods. This impacts not only trade execution but tracking error—the deviation between an ETF's performance and the index it seeks to replicate.

Tracking error, while often ignored, is a meaningful cost over time. It can arise from several sources: imperfect replication (e.g. sampling instead of full replication), trading costs within the fund, dividend timing mismatches, or foreign exchange fluctuations. A fund that lags its benchmark by 0.2% annually due to structural drag is delivering a worse result than its index promises, even if its expense ratio is low. In that sense, *low fees are only half the story—efficient tracking completes the picture.*

Tax efficiency is another dimension where ETFs typically outperform mutual funds, particularly in the United States and increasingly in other jurisdictions. The in-kind creation and redemption mechanism allows ETFs to manage capital gains distributions far more effectively. When investors in a mutual fund redeem their shares, the manager may need to sell securities to meet redemptions, potentially triggering taxable gains for remaining shareholders. ETFs, by contrast, can offload low-basis securities through the redemption process without realising gains within the fund. This structural advantage doesn't show up in the expense ratio—but it directly affects after-tax returns.

However, tax drag is not eliminated entirely. Investors still face taxation on dividends, and certain ETF structures (such as those using synthetic replication or domiciled in different jurisdictions) may create unexpected tax implications. A UK investor buying a US-domiciled ETF, for instance, may be subject to a 15% withholding tax on dividends, even inside an ISA or SIPP. Conversely, an Ireland-domiciled ETF holding US stocks often reduces this withholding to 15% at the fund level, passing on improved yield to the investor. Understanding domicile, tax treaties, and reporting standards can significantly improve net outcomes. It requires diligence—not just in choosing the right fund, but in understanding how and where it operates.

The final layer of cost—though perhaps the most dangerous—is behavioural. The indirect friction of frequent switching, tactical reallocations, or style chasing can erode performance far more than fees ever will. Studies have consistently shown that the average investor underperforms their own investments due to poor timing decisions. They buy after strong performance, sell after dips, and shift strategies in search of novelty. Even low-cost ETFs cannot defend against this behavioural tax. In fact, the very liquidity that makes ETFs attractive can become a liability when it tempts overtrading. *A 0.05% fee is insignificant next to a 5% panic sale.*

This is where intentional portfolio design plays a protective role. By choosing ETFs that align with long-term strategy, reducing overlap, and automating contributions or rebalancing, investors can limit the opportunities for self-sabotage. A passive portfolio, properly constructed, should require minimal maintenance—not because it's simplistic, but because its underlying mechanics remove the need for constant adjustment. Cost control is not only about selecting the cheapest products; it is about reducing the *frequency and friction of decisions.* Inattention to this fact can quietly erode the most elegantly designed portfolio.

Moreover, fee structures are evolving. The rise of actively managed ETFs introduces new pricing layers, sometimes with performance-based fees or higher baseline expenses. Some of these funds deliver value—through risk-adjusted strategies, factor tilts, or thematic insights—but their cost must be weighed against replicable alternatives. Likewise, smart beta products, which promise index-like transparency with performance-enhancing factors, often come at a premium. These innovations are not inherently flawed, but they demand scrutiny. A high-fee fund may be justifiable, but never *by default.* It must earn its place through clarity, precision, and documented efficacy—not marketing.

Ultimately, investors don't lose returns all at once. They forfeit them gradually—through fractions of a percent, misplaced trust, misaligned products, or a failure to re-examine what once seemed adequate. The most dangerous costs are rarely loud. They are hidden in plain sight, deducted silently year after year, just enough to go unnoticed, but relentless enough to reshape outcomes over time. Inattention to cost is not benign—it is a slow betrayal of the investor's intention.

Mastering the cost dimension of investing is not about becoming a zealot for the lowest possible fee. It is about recognising that small differences *compound*, that structure matters, and that simplicity—when paired with scrutiny—is often the most powerful strategy available. A portfolio is not only a reflection of beliefs and goals; it is a system. And every system has friction. The question is whether that friction is necessary, understood, and managed—or merely ignored. For thoughtful investors, that distinction may be the most important basis point of all.

Chapter 3
The Psychology Portfolio

Every investor, sooner or later, comes to a startling realisation: the greatest threat to their wealth is rarely the market itself. Not inflation, interest rates, or geopolitical upheavals—but the persistent, invisible tug of human psychology. The instincts that once safeguarded our ancestors—urgency in crises, loss aversion, confidence in our own judgement—now work against us in markets built around patience and probability. This chapter confronts that reality head-on. Not with guilt, nor with abstraction, but with insight that allows the investor to design around human frailty rather than deny it.

Markets are more than systems of capital allocation; they are emotional amplifiers. Two individuals may hold identical assets, with identical allocations, yet one panics during a downturn and sells, while the other maintains discipline. Success here is less about intellect than about temperament. The capacity to endure volatility without abandoning a plan often outweighs the ability to analyse balance sheets.

This can be a bitter pill for the intelligent. Smart investors are not immune; indeed, intelligence often compounds behavioural error. More information is mistakenly equated with better decisions. Complexity is mistaken for insight; activity for control. Market narratives seduce the confident, shaping behaviour less through facts than through subconscious biases. Anchoring to past highs, overestimating rare events, interpreting randomness as trend—these are not failures of the uninformed; they are default wiring of the human mind quietly distorting judgement in real time.

Loss aversion is perhaps the most potent and least appreciated bias. Research shows that losses are felt about twice as acutely as equivalent gains. A £1,000 dip hurts far more than a £1,000 gain satisfies. This asymmetry drives risk avoidance in declining markets, premature selling to "lock in" gains, and fixation on avoiding loss at the cost of forgoing opportunity. Left unchecked, such distortions quietly erode returns, compromising financial goals.

Merely recognising these biases is insufficient. Awareness does not confer immunity. What is required is design—a portfolio architecture that anticipates human behaviour and erects safeguards against self-sabotage. The most effective investors do not suppress emotion by force; they construct systems that prevent impulsive missteps.

Enter the psychology portfolio. Not a formula or model, but a mindset rooted in realism about human behaviour under stress. Many mathematically "optimal" portfolios fail in practice because they are psychologically unliveable. A 90% equity allocation may maximise expected returns, but if it prompts panic during a 30% drawdown, it is not just ineffective—it is destructive. Rational plans are only effective if they can be followed when irrationality strikes.

The previously introduced "boring" portfolio finds its strongest justification here. What seems dull in calm markets often feels agonising in turmoil. Yet simplicity is strength when volatility reigns. A rules-based ETF allocation reduces the noise that triggers reactive behaviour, focusing the investor on controllable factors: allocation, costs, and time horizon. Emotionally survivable portfolios are more likely to be held long enough to compound; theoretically optimised ones often crumble under pressure.

Even the best plans remain vulnerable at decision points. Automation is not mere convenience—it is strategic discipline. Automating contributions, rebalancing, and even investment choices removes the constant need for reaffirming intent, reducing opportunities for emotion-driven deviation. Many view automation as disengagement, but it is precommitment: ensuring that best intentions persist when instincts protest. Set a globally diversified ETF allocation on autopilot, and future markets no longer demand courage or insight—the decision has already been made.

This is not a one-size-fits-all prescription. The psychology portfolio is about alignment, not replication. Knowing yourself—your tendencies, anxieties, and risk appetite—is central. Do you check markets daily? Do drawdowns provoke panic? Do you prefer smoother returns at the cost of upside, or thrive on volatility?

Answers determine whether a portfolio survives turbulence or invites constant intervention.

A minimalist investor may thrive with two or three funds—global equities, bonds, and liquidity. Another might employ factor tilts, satellite holdings, or tactical shifts. The goal is not prescription, but fit. A portfolio must accommodate real-world behaviour, not idealised intentions. Otherwise, every drawdown tests faith; every divergence prompts ill-considered adjustments. Each deviation chips away at compounding.

Here, a subtle but vital distinction arises: risk tolerance differs from risk capacity. A young investor may have decades to recover from volatility (capacity), yet lack the temperament (tolerance). A retiree may feel emotionally comfortable with equities but cannot absorb a major drawdown. Psychology, more than theory, governs outcomes when markets turn. Risk is as much about internal reaction as external movement.

This chapter does not aim to "fix" investor psychology—that is neither feasible nor necessary. Instead, it integrates psychology into portfolio design, illustrating why even the most intelligent investors make predictable errors when markets accelerate. Anchoring, loss aversion, and overconfidence quietly erode returns. The tools offered here automate discipline without sacrificing intention, supporting portfolios that are practical and psychologically durable.

The objective is not perfection, but durability. A portfolio you can trust amid screaming headlines. A system that keeps you invested not because you feel confident, but because structure obviates impulsive decisions. A plan reflecting goals and limits alike. This is the psychology portfolio—less about outsmarting others, more about aligning with your own human tendencies to stay invested long enough for compounding to work its quiet magic.

You need not become a different person to succeed. You must, however, stop expecting rational action under stress unless it is engineered into your process. In markets, as in life, structure trumps willpower. When that structure mirrors true psychology, you vastly increase the likelihood of achieving what most investors never do:

staying the course long enough to let compounding quietly do its work. This chapter is about building that structure deliberately, clearly, and with respect for the human mind under uncertainty.

Why Smart People Make Dumb Investing Decisions

The most sophisticated threat to an investor's success is not ignorance, but confidence untethered from self-awareness. Time and again, intelligent individuals—armed with data, credentials, and conviction—make decisions in markets that, with hindsight, defy logic. Not because they lacked information or skill, but because they were ambushed by their own psychology. *The mind is not a neutral observer in markets; it is an active, unpredictable participant—interpreting randomness as pattern, framing losses as threats, and mistaking recent events for timeless truths.* In investing, intelligence does not guarantee immunity from error. If anything, it often increases exposure to it.

What makes this reality so problematic is that the very people who are most confident in their decision-making are often the most vulnerable to systematic cognitive errors. This is not a critique of character or ability—it is a documented consequence of how the brain processes uncertainty and risk. Academic literature, particularly in behavioural finance, is clear: the smarter you are, the better you are at rationalising irrational decisions. You don't avoid mistakes; you justify them with greater sophistication.

Take overconfidence. Among the most pervasive behavioural biases, overconfidence leads investors to overestimate their ability to select outperforming assets, time the market, or "see the signal" before others do. It's not limited to novices. In fact, it increases with education and expertise. Professional investors are particularly prone to it, in part because their environments reward certainty and penalise hesitation. But certainty is not the same as correctness. Studies consistently show that active fund managers, despite their expertise, underperform broad indices over long timeframes—often due to excessive trading and misplaced conviction. *Believing you have an edge does not create one. It merely exposes you to the cost of being wrong more often than you realise.*

Another invisible saboteur is anchoring: the tendency to fixate on arbitrary reference points, usually without awareness. A stock that was once worth £80 but now trades at £60 "feels cheap," even if its fair value is £40. A portfolio that was once worth £500,000 but has fallen to £450,000 "feels like a loss," even though the money invested may still be in positive territory overall. These emotional benchmarks have no bearing on future outcomes, yet they influence decisions as if they do. Investors anchored to previous highs often hold onto losing positions in the hope of a return to "break even," rather than reassessing the investment's merits objectively. This inertia results not from rational analysis, but from emotional discomfort with accepting a loss.

Then there's loss aversion—a bias so potent it can override both logic and probability. People dislike losses far more than they enjoy equivalent gains, often by a factor of two or more. This asymmetry doesn't merely make investors risk-averse; it distorts their entire frame of reference. In declining markets, portfolios are liquidated not based on long-term thinking, but to avoid the visceral pain of watching numbers fall. Conversely, gains are often locked in prematurely, with investors cashing out winners to "protect profits," even when fundamentals justify holding. *The result is a paradox: portfolios are de-risked during downturns, missing recoveries, and over-risked during euphoric rallies, chasing diminishing returns.*

These behaviours are not minor errors. They are compounding liabilities. Over time, they erode performance more effectively than high fees or poor timing. They are the psychological equivalent of hidden costs—rarely itemised, never explicit, but ever-present. And perhaps most dangerous of all is that they tend to be invisible in real time. We don't notice that we're being irrational; we experience our reactions as justified, urgent, even prudent. The problem is not the feeling itself. The problem is acting on it without scrutiny.

There's a particular irony to the fact that financial literacy alone does little to prevent these mistakes. In many cases, it reinforces them. Knowledge breeds confidence, but confidence untethered from self-reflection becomes its own risk factor. The economist who can recite Fama-French factors but still panics during a 15% drawdown. The tech executive who built a fortune on innovation but holds 90% of their wealth in a single company. The data analyst who obsesses over charts but fails to stay invested during a bear market. Intelligence, when not paired with emotional awareness, simply sharpens the tools of self-deception.

So what, then, is the remedy? Not more data. Not more market commentary. Certainly not more complex strategy. The remedy is *structure*—rules-based investing, behavioural guardrails, and intentional design that anticipates psychological failure points and limits the damage they can do. Automated ETF investing, as explored elsewhere in this book, is not a shortcut for lazy investors. It is an intelligent defence against overconfidence, anchoring, and loss aversion. It replaces the need for moment-to-moment decision-making with systems that compound over time regardless of emotional weather.

And yet, even structural discipline is vulnerable if the investor remains unaware of how these biases operate. This is why behavioural insight must sit alongside financial knowledge. It's not enough to know what a diversified portfolio looks like. You must understand why you might abandon it. It's not enough to understand historical drawdowns. You must anticipate how they will *feel*—and how that feeling might drive you to override your plan. *Investment success is not about eliminating emotion, but about reducing its ability to distort decision-making.*

This insight is particularly crucial in moments of market stress, when headlines escalate fear and social proof reinforces reactive behaviour. When markets fall sharply, most investors look around—not to reassess fundamentals, but to see what others are doing. This herd behaviour creates a dangerous loop: panic leads to selling, selling leads to further price drops, and those drops validate the original fear. The investor who can detach from this loop—not through superiority, but through pre-committed design—is the one most likely to benefit from future recoveries.

Contrary to popular belief, most investing mistakes are not born of greed. They are born of *fear*—fear of missing out, fear of losing what's been gained, fear of being wrong, or of being left behind. Smart people are especially susceptible because they believe they should be in control. Markets punish that belief. They are probabilistic, not deterministic. They do not reward brilliance if it comes untethered from humility. And they certainly do not care about your goals or your narrative. They behave as they behave—and the investor's task is not to outwit them, but to endure them without self-sabotage.

One of the most important mental shifts an investor can make is from performance-chasing to error-avoidance. The former is alluring, but fragile. The latter is boring, but durable. Avoiding the big mistake—panic selling, overtrading, chasing trends, abandoning the plan—is often more impactful than making the perfect tactical decision. But this only becomes clear with time. In the short term, the brilliant investor appears impressive. In the long term, the disciplined one tends to win.

This chapter section exists not to pathologise human behaviour, but to clarify it. You are not irrational because you make these mistakes. You are human. But if you fail to recognise these invisible forces—anchoring, overconfidence, loss aversion—you will build portfolios vulnerable to the worst of your instincts. Awareness is the starting point. Structure is the remedy. And time, protected from interference, is the ultimate asset.

If there is one takeaway worth remembering, it is this: *investing is not a test of knowledge, but of behaviour.* Mastery does not belong to the smartest investor, but to the one most aligned with reality—both the market's, and their own.

The Need for a Boring Plan

The investing world is saturated with complexity masquerading as sophistication. We're encouraged to believe that intricate models, dynamic allocations, and continual adjustments reflect financial maturity. But this mindset often betrays a deeper insecurity—the belief that action equals control. What most investors fail to appreciate is that *the most resilient portfolios are not the ones that impress during market highs, but the ones that can survive the lows without being abandoned.* This is where a boring plan becomes not just a practical tool but a profound strategic advantage.

A rational portfolio is easy to design on a spreadsheet. You balance risk and return expectations, plot historical drawdowns, run Monte Carlo simulations, and end up with an elegant asset mix that optimises long-term growth. But the real test is never on paper—it is in the living, breathing markets where volatility is visceral, narratives shift overnight, and losses feel personal. *A plan that's rational but emotionally unsustainable is a liability, not a strategy.* It lulls you into a false sense of preparedness until the first real storm hits.

The allure of complexity is particularly dangerous for intelligent investors. They often mistake understanding for preparedness. But understanding that a 30% drawdown is statistically normal doesn't mean you'll remain calm when it happens to your own capital. Knowing that equities rebound over time doesn't immunise you from fear when headlines scream crisis. This disconnection between intellectual knowledge and emotional experience is where many investors stumble. They had a plan—but not one they could live with.

The antidote is boring. Not simplistic, not lazy—boring. A boring plan is one that is *built for endurance.* It anticipates your own behavioural tendencies, accounts for your emotional triggers, and prioritises sustainability over optimisation. It might not be the most efficient on paper, but it's designed to be held through the parts of the market cycle that matter most: the downturns.

Consider the psychology of a 60/40 portfolio. It's often ridiculed for being outdated or suboptimal in the modern market landscape. Yet it remains one of the most resilient allocations for a reason: it blends growth potential with ballast. It might not shoot the lights out during bull runs, but it rarely triggers the kind of panic that leads to self-sabotage. For many investors, that kind of psychological stability *outperforms* more aggressive strategies over time, because it avoids the behavioural cost of abandonment.

This is not about advocating one allocation over another. It is about acknowledging that the right portfolio is not the one that looks best in backtests—it's the one that *survives your own psychology*. For some, a higher equity allocation is tolerable. For others, even moderate volatility is a stressor. Knowing this about yourself is more valuable than any forecast or model. It allows you to design not just for returns, but for *resilience.*

This is where emotional self-awareness becomes a financial skill. How did you react during the March 2020 sell-off? Or the tech bust of 2001? Or the financial crisis in 2008? Did you hold steady, reallocate, or retreat to cash? Your answers to these questions should shape your portfolio more than any market outlook. Because when the next downturn arrives—and it will—your response will not be a function of knowledge. It will be a function of your *emotional design.*

Automating your investment process is one way to enforce that design. Regular contributions into a low-cost ETF portfolio with fixed asset allocations removes the need for continual decision-making. It creates rhythm, not reactivity. More importantly, it builds a habit of disinterest in short-term movements. You stop checking your portfolio weekly because there's nothing to do. This is not passivity—it's pre-emptive discipline. *By reducing optionality, you reduce volatility of behaviour—arguably the most important variable in long-term outcomes.*

The obsession with maximising returns is often a mask for discomfort with stillness. Investors seek complexity because they equate activity with progress. But the data are clear: long-term performance is far more sensitive to behaviour than to selection. A portfolio held through cycles compounds far more effectively than one that is constantly adjusted in response to noise. In other words, *the investor who sticks with a boring plan usually beats the one chasing brilliance.*

There is a deeper philosophical insight here. Investing is not just a financial activity—it is a test of character. When markets fall, the temptation is not merely to change strategy—it is to find emotional relief. Selling in a panic is not a financial error so much as a psychological coping mechanism. A boring plan, by removing the need for interpretation and discretion, *protects you from yourself.* It absorbs the pressure to act by making action irrelevant.

This does not mean never reviewing or adjusting your strategy. It means designing one that requires *very few decisions*, and only under calm conditions. It means decoupling the plan from the news cycle, the daily charts, and the endless flow of macro predictions. You are not a fund manager reporting to clients. You are a long-term investor with a clear set of goals. *You don't need to outperform the market—you need to outlast your own worst instincts.*

And yet, there is resistance. "Surely I can do better than just buying and holding broad-market ETFs." Perhaps. But the better question is: *Can you do better consistently, without succumbing to fatigue, distraction, or emotional interference?* If the answer is no—and for most, it is—then complexity becomes a tax, not a feature.

The paradox is that most investors don't want boring until they've experienced the cost of not having it. After several cycles of overreaction, chasing returns, switching strategies, and realising too late that the market doesn't reward cleverness as much as it rewards consistency, they begin to appreciate the calm power of simplicity. But this wisdom is expensive if it comes only through trial and error. *Far better to begin with a plan designed for your temperament, rather than reverse-engineer one after multiple disappointments.*

There's no shortage of tools, funds, or models to help construct an elegant portfolio. But few of these tools ask the most important questions: What level of volatility can you tolerate without changing course? What asset allocation will allow you to sleep during market stress? What habits protect you from impulsive decisions? These are not technical queries—they are behavioural diagnostics. And they are more predictive of long-term success than any performance metric.

Ultimately, a boring plan is an act of financial maturity. It reflects the recognition that your edge lies not in forecasting, but in staying power. It rejects the allure of complexity, not out of ignorance, but out of clarity. It is a plan built to be *kept*, not just admired. It is not designed to excite, but to endure.

The best investors are not necessarily the smartest—they are the ones who *need the fewest interventions*. Their portfolios reflect discipline, not drama. Their strategy does not change with every headline. And most importantly, their plans are not just rational—they are *livable*. That is what makes boring beautiful. That is what makes it powerful.

Automation as Liberation

Investing, at its core, is not just a financial decision—it is a behavioural one. The most reliable predictor of long-term performance is not stock selection, market timing, or economic forecasting. It is whether the investor can avoid getting in their own way. Automation, when deployed with intention, is not a tool of the disengaged—it is the defence mechanism of the self-aware. It allows us to sidestep the traps of emotion, impulse, and fatigue. *It is not abdication of control—it is refinement of control.*

Every investing decision we leave to discretion is an invitation for irrationality. Whether to buy now or wait, to increase contributions this month or delay them, to rebalance or ride the trend—each decision point introduces vulnerability. Behavioural economics has mapped the contours of these vulnerabilities in exquisite detail: loss aversion, recency bias, action bias, overconfidence, and countless others. The academic insights are familiar, but the consequences are deeply personal. We know what we should do, but we frequently do the opposite—especially when the stakes feel high. Automation is the quiet solution that removes the temptation before it arrives.

Dollar-cost averaging is one of the most effective examples of this principle. Automatically investing a fixed amount into a diversified ETF portfolio at regular intervals—weekly, monthly, or quarterly—removes the need to 'wait for a better entry point' or worry about timing. It also exploits volatility rather than fearing it. When prices are down, the same investment buys more units; when prices are high, it buys fewer. Over time, this disciplines the investor into accumulating assets through all phases of the market cycle without overthinking any single move. It transforms investing from an episodic act of willpower into a systemic, continuous habit.

But the power of automation goes beyond cashflow scheduling. It extends to allocation and rebalancing. Portfolios drift. Equity markets outpace bonds, certain sectors surge while others lag, and emotional attachment to winners builds silently. Left unchecked, these drifts distort the original risk profile and amplify exposure to unintended concentrations. A well-automated system doesn't just invest regularly—it periodically restores balance. Rebalancing ensures that the portfolio maintains its intended shape, even as markets move unpredictably. Without it, long-term performance becomes a hostage to whichever asset class is enjoying temporary favour.

Automation also addresses a more subtle but critical challenge: cognitive bandwidth. The modern investor is overwhelmed with information—market updates, economic data, expert commentary, algorithmic noise. Amidst this deluge, the ability to focus on long-term objectives weakens. Automation restores focus by *filtering out the irrelevant.* If your investment schedule is fixed, if your allocation is maintained, if your strategy is pre-defined, then ninety percent of market news becomes moot. This frees up cognitive energy for decisions that actually matter—career development, financial planning, or simply living with less financial anxiety.

Consider the experience of retirement savers who auto-enrol into pension schemes with target-date funds. These products automatically adjust asset allocation as the investor ages—reducing risk gradually over time. Despite their simplicity, studies consistently show that participants in such schemes outperform those who self-manage, not because the allocations are superior, but because *the behaviour is superior*. Participation rates are higher. Contribution levels increase steadily. Withdrawal patterns are more disciplined. All because the system is structured to make the optimal behaviour the default behaviour.

There is a temptation among ambitious investors to reject automation as too pedestrian—as if handing over control is equivalent to settling for mediocrity. But this view mistakes *discretion for intelligence*. The investor who insists on constant intervention must beat not just the market, but their own behavioural inconsistencies. Few succeed at this over decades. In contrast, the investor who automates contributions, holds diversified ETFs, and rebalances mechanically is not passive—they are pre-committed. Their edge is not cleverness, but *consistency*.

This is especially relevant during periods of market stress. When volatility spikes, headlines scream, and the consensus mood swings from exuberance to despair, human judgement becomes erratic. Some investors freeze. Others panic-sell. Many abandon their plan. Automated systems, however, don't panic. They don't seek reassurance or second-guess the news cycle. They execute. This emotional neutrality is one of the most underappreciated assets in a long-term investing strategy.

There is a philosophical clarity to this approach as well. Automation forces an investor to confront their values and codify their intent in advance. What am I saving for? What level of risk am I truly comfortable with? How often will I review my plan—and what circumstances would justify change? These are difficult questions. They require honest self-assessment. But once answered, they become the blueprint for a system that *enforces those answers*. The investor becomes accountable not to the market, but to their own principles.

None of this means that automation eliminates the need for review. It is not a set-it-and-forget-it dogma. Circumstances change. Goals evolve. Life stages bring new priorities. But the difference is this: *reviews are conducted from a place of calm, not crisis*. They are scheduled, not reactive. They are intentional, not impulsive. Automation creates the space for reflection by insulating the investor from the noise between reviews.

There is also an ethical dimension to consider. In a culture that romanticises hustle and glorifies control, choosing automation is a quiet rebellion. It says: I will not allow markets to dictate my time, my emotions, or my energy. I will design a system that serves me—not the other way around. It reflects a deeper form of agency—*the decision to step back, not out of apathy, but out of strategic clarity.*

Critics may argue that automation introduces rigidity or reduces optionality. But structure is not the enemy of freedom—disorganisation is. By automating the repetitive, emotionally charged decisions, we reclaim attention for higher-order thinking. We move from reacting to designing. From fearing volatility to embracing process. From chasing returns to compounding discipline.

There is a reason that the most successful investment firms rely on systems, not spontaneity. Institutions automate because they cannot afford to rely on mood or intuition. Individuals have even more reason to do so—because they are more emotionally exposed, less diversified across mandates, and more likely to make decisions under stress. What institutions do out of necessity, individuals should do out of *prudence.*

In the long run, automation is not about achieving the highest theoretical return. It is about achieving *the return you will actually capture.* That return is not defined by market conditions alone, but by whether you stay invested through the hard years. The system that helps you stay in the game—unshaken, uninterrupted, and unburdened—is the system that wins.

And that is the real liberation. Not the freedom to make more decisions, but the freedom *from needing to make them.* Not the thrill of tactical agility, but the peace of strategic conviction. Automation is not mechanical. It is intentional. It is not emotionless. It is emotionally intelligent. It is not about doing less. It is about doing what matters—and doing it relentlessly well.

Designing a Portfolio You'll Actually Keep

The success of any investment strategy lies not in its theoretical superiority but in its psychological durability. A perfect portfolio on paper is worthless if it cannot be held through uncertainty, drawdowns, or disillusionment. The markets will, without fail, test every investor's resolve. Fear will creep in during corrections, envy will rise during rallies, and doubt will linger in long flat periods. The only portfolios that succeed are those that survive these tests—not just financially, but emotionally. *The best portfolio is not the one with the highest expected return; it is the one you are most likely to keep holding when it matters most.*

The illusion of the optimal portfolio seduces many investors. We run simulations, compare historical performance, optimise based on Sharpe ratios or downside risk metrics. These are useful tools, but they often ignore the single most important variable in long-term wealth-building: *your own tolerance for discomfort.* Markets will fluctuate, sometimes violently. Your portfolio must be built not for the idealised version of yourself—the one who's calm, rational, and detached—but for the real version who will check their balance after a 20% drop and wonder whether to abandon the plan altogether.

Understanding one's psychological risk profile is not an admission of weakness. It is a strategic necessity. The investor who underestimates their capacity for loss typically makes the same mistake repeatedly: stretching into higher-risk allocations during euphoric periods, then panic-selling during downturns. This is not a failure of intellect; it is a misreading of temperament. Designing a portfolio that reflects your true emotional threshold is the difference between consistency and chaos. This is not about lowering your ambition. *It is about respecting the behavioural limits that govern your actions in the real world.*

For the conservative investor, safety is not just a preference—it is a precondition for participation. A portfolio weighted heavily towards bonds, high-quality dividend-paying ETFs, or low-volatility factor strategies can offer a sense of security. This may not maximise returns in bull markets, but it enhances the likelihood of staying invested across cycles. Importantly, conservative portfolios are not synonymous with passive neglect. They still require careful construction, diversification, and cost efficiency. But their defining characteristic is that they reduce the emotional pain of watching one's investments lose value—a pain that, if not managed, often leads to unwise decisions.

On the opposite end is the aggressive investor—someone with a longer time horizon, higher risk tolerance, and a greater stomach for drawdowns. This individual may favour equity-heavy ETF allocations, emerging market exposures, or thematic sectors aligned with disruptive innovation. But even within this aggressive framework, the structure must still be stable. Volatility is not an issue if it is expected and internalised. The real danger arises when risk is misunderstood—when it shows up as a surprise rather than a cost of doing business. The aggressive portfolio works best when the investor has been honest about the level of pain they are willing to endure before reacting emotionally.

There is also a third archetype—what might be called the minimalist investor. This person does not wish to monitor markets, track shifting asset class correlations, or make quarterly rebalancing decisions. They want a simple, scalable plan that can run quietly in the background. For this investor, one or two globally diversified ETFs—perhaps an all-in-one fund or a blend of equity and bond ETFs—can serve as the entire portfolio. Minimalist portfolios are not simplistic; they are sophisticated in their restraint. Their strength lies in reducing decision fatigue. *When complexity goes down, consistency often goes up.*

Choosing among these styles requires more than knowing your age or income. It requires an honest confrontation with how you respond to uncertainty. One useful exercise is to mentally walk through market scenarios. What would you do if your portfolio declined 30%? Would you continue investing, hold steady, or pull out? What if a colleague boasts about outsized returns in speculative assets? Would you feel compelled to chase? Would you change course mid-cycle if your portfolio underperforms for a year? These are not theoretical questions. They are diagnostic tools. *They reveal the triggers that will test your discipline—and help you build around them, not in defiance of them.*

ETF-based portfolios lend themselves especially well to this kind of psychological alignment. They are modular. They can be adjusted easily to reflect risk appetite, time horizon, or philosophical orientation—whether that means ESG-conscious investing, regional tilts, or factor exposures. ETFs also provide transparency. You can see exactly what you own, in real time. This visibility matters. *Ambiguity increases anxiety.* When you understand the composition and purpose of your holdings, you are more likely to stick with them through periods of doubt.

The decision about how to construct your portfolio should begin with the following premise: the portfolio must match not only your financial goals, but your cognitive and emotional architecture. Do not adopt an aggressive portfolio because the internet suggests you should "maximise compounding." Do not adopt a conservative one because a pundit warns of an impending crash. Build a system that reflects your beliefs, supports your temperament, and removes the need for constant vigilance. This is not about tailoring the market to your mood. It is about tailoring your exposure to your endurance.

Behavioural finance research has consistently shown that investors tend to *overestimate their ability to endure losses* and *underestimate their tendency to react emotionally under pressure.* This mismatch is what destroys long-term returns—not the asset allocation itself, but the interruptions, the impulsive reallocations, and the abandonment of strategy at precisely the wrong time. The antidote is not a perfect formula. It is a system designed around behavioural realism.

One of the most powerful ways to achieve this is through scenario-based stress testing. Before committing to any asset mix, imagine its performance in historical crises. How would it have fared during the Global Financial Crisis? The COVID crash? The dot-com bust? What drawdowns would it have incurred, and over what duration would recovery have occurred? Then ask yourself: *Would you have stayed invested?* Not the version of you reading this book, but the version checking your brokerage account in a moment of panic. That version—the one with a racing heart and mounting doubt—is the one that determines outcomes.

A well-designed portfolio is therefore not just financially sound—it is *psychologically survivable.* It limits the need for mid-course corrections. It creates emotional stability through strategic clarity. And it turns investing into a process, not a performance. Once this architecture is in place, your primary job becomes not tinkering with the portfolio, but continuing to fund it, automate it, and *ignore the temptation to re-evaluate it too frequently.*

Ultimately, a portfolio is not a monument to your intelligence. It is a reflection of your self-awareness. It is the container that holds your ambition, your fears, your biases, and your habits. And if it is designed well—designed not just for theoretical efficiency but for real-world behaviour—it becomes more than just a collection of financial instruments. *It becomes a partner in your long-term success.* One that doesn't demand brilliance or foresight, only that you keep showing up, with consistency, through all market conditions.

This is the quiet power of alignment. When your portfolio fits you—truly fits you—it does not feel like a burden. It does not provoke anxiety every time markets dip or headlines flare. It feels natural. Sustainable. Quietly effective. Not because it's the best possible portfolio, but because it's the one you'll actually keep.

Chapter 4
Choosing the Right ETF — Filters, Not FOMO

At first blush, exchange-traded funds appear almost disarmingly simple. Pick a ticker, click 'buy', and instantly gain exposure to a diversified basket of assets. Yet beneath that apparent ease lies a subtler reality: not all ETFs are created equal. Even those with nearly identical names can diverge in performance in ways that only a discerning eye will catch. This chapter is about lifting the hood—dispassionately, methodically—to examine what you are really buying. It is about choosing based on structure, fit, and function rather than popularity or promise, about filtering out noise rather than feeding your FOMO.

The ETF landscape is crowded, noisy, and ever-expanding. Week by week, new offerings emerge, targeting ever-narrower slices of the market: "Millennial Innovation", "Pet Economy", "Space Exploration". Some of these products are genuinely useful tools; many are little more than speculative theatre. Without careful discernment, investors risk mistaking novelty for strategy—or worse, confusing entertainment for disciplined portfolio design.

This chapter aims to cultivate that discernment. Our goal is not merely to identify "good" ETFs but to guide readers towards selections aligned with a broader philosophy of ownership, risk tolerance, and portfolio purpose. We explore subtle yet significant variations among seemingly similar funds, considering tracking error, fund structure, and sponsor quality—not as trivia, but as variables that materially affect outcomes. A ticker symbol is shorthand, not truth.

Awareness is the starting point. Many retail investors assume that two ETFs tracking the same index—say, the S&P 500—are interchangeable. In practice, differences in replication method, expense ratio, securities lending practices, and governance can lead to measurable divergence over time. Some ETFs employ full replication; others opt for optimisation. Some are open-ended funds;

others are unit investment trusts. These design choices carry implications for tax efficiency, liquidity, and index fidelity, especially during volatile periods.

Take two ETFs tracking the NASDAQ-100. Their top holdings—Apple, Microsoft, Amazon—may appear identical. Yet one may rely on synthetic replication while the other purchases actual securities. One may engage in more securities lending, subtly affecting returns; another may reinvest dividends differently or manage corporate actions with greater precision. Over years, these operational nuances compound into meaningful differences. ETF selection, therefore, is less about exposure than about execution.

This is not pedantry; it is intelligent investing. Moving from label-reading to substance-weighing allows long-term investors to resist chasing yield, to endure periods of underperformance, and to stay committed to plans grounded in clarity.

Volume and liquidity deserve equal scrutiny. Assets under management are often misinterpreted: high AUM can signal confidence—or merely reflect past hype. Trading volume hints at liquidity, but only when considered alongside bid-ask spreads, market-maker activity, and the underlying securities. A high-volume ETF holding illiquid assets may still experience slippage under stress; conversely, a low-volume ETF tracking a broad index may trade smoothly thanks to efficient underlying liquidity and arbitrage mechanisms. Context, not surface metrics, matters.

The lure of niche ETFs presents another challenge. Thematic funds—blockchain, cannabis, genomics—offer access to bold ideas but can be poorly diversified, illiquid, and costly. Not inherently flawed, they are simply specialised. They have a place in a portfolio, but only with moderation and a clear understanding of their role. This is where our classification framework becomes invaluable.

The Three-Bucket Test provides a simple mental model: Core, Satellite, Speculative. Core ETFs form the foundation—broad-based, low-cost, designed for permanence. Satellite ETFs are targeted, often thematic, employed to tilt a portfolio. Speculative ETFs are high-volatility bets, capable of spectacular gains or sudden loss. Placing holdings into these buckets enforces discipline, reduces overlap, and clarifies purpose: why exactly are you holding this fund?

Many investors struggle to answer that. They know what they bought, but rarely why. Is it redundant with another fund? Is it overpriced relative to its contribution? Does it complement or contradict risk tolerance? Classifying ETFs transforms passive collectors into active curators. And with that shift comes confidence—not flamboyance, but the quiet assurance that choices are deliberate and portfolios reflect clarity rather than chaos.

ETF investing is often portrayed as plug-and-play. The simplicity narrative sells. But simplicity must not replace discernment. Here, we raise the standard—not by adding complexity, but by refining awareness. Understanding the instrument beneath the ticker stops you chasing the crowd and begins the work of investing with intention.

This chapter aims to move you from reaction to reasoning. From grabbing the latest thematic ETF to appreciating enduring truths of long-term investing. By its end, you will not only know how to filter ETFs with intelligence—you will see how those filters reinforce a broader philosophy. Choosing an ETF is no longer just about potential returns; it is about choosing clarity. And clarity, unlike FOMO, compounds quietly over time.

Look Under the Hood, Not Just the Label

The illusion of sameness is one of the most persistent traps in modern investing. It's easy to assume that two ETFs tracking the same index—say, the FTSE 100 or the S&P 500—must be essentially interchangeable. After all, if they hold the same underlying assets, shouldn't they deliver the same results? This superficial logic is appealing. It's also dangerously incomplete. In reality, the differences between seemingly identical ETFs can be both subtle and consequential, often hiding in the operational details, cost structures, and governance choices that the average investor never sees. Yet those very differences can have an outsized effect on long-term performance, tax efficiency, and the integrity of your investment strategy.

At its core, this subchapter is about cultivating discernment—learning to evaluate ETFs not just by what they say they track, but by how they're built, maintained, and managed. The ETF market, now a multitrillion-dollar ecosystem, is no longer defined solely by exposure. Execution matters. Structure matters. Sponsor quality matters. And the ability to distinguish between a well-constructed fund and a mediocre imitation may mean the difference between quietly compounding wealth and unknowingly leaking returns over decades.

To begin, let's examine tracking error—one of the most underappreciated metrics in ETF selection. Tracking error measures the deviation between an ETF's returns and the returns of its underlying index. While some deviation is inevitable due to fees and operational friction, persistent or unexplained divergence can be a red flag. A fund that consistently underperforms its benchmark by more than its expense ratio suggests something deeper may be at play: poor replication methodology, inefficient rebalancing, or even lax risk controls. Two ETFs tracking the same index might publish identical top holdings, but one may rebalance quarterly while the other adjusts daily. One may use full physical replication; the other, a sampling approach. Over time, these structural choices can accumulate into meaningfully different results.

Consider two S&P 500 ETFs—one from a large, established issuer like Vanguard or iShares, and another from a smaller, lesser-known provider. On the surface, both track the same benchmark and hold the same names. But look closer. The first might benefit from economies of scale, tighter bid-ask spreads, and superior securities lending practices that generate extra revenue returned to shareholders. The second might suffer from wider spreads, less effective replication, and higher internal turnover, all of which eat into net performance. *ETF selection is not about the label—it is about operational excellence.*

Another often-overlooked factor is fund structure. ETFs can be organised in several different ways—open-ended funds, unit investment trusts, grantor trusts, partnerships—and each carries unique implications. For example, synthetic ETFs use derivatives rather than owning physical securities. While these structures can offer exposure to hard-to-access markets and lower costs, they also introduce counterparty risk and greater complexity. For investors seeking simplicity and transparency, these features may be unwelcome. Meanwhile, certain ETFs are domiciled in jurisdictions with different tax treatments, affecting how dividends are paid or whether withholdings apply to foreign investors. *A ticker may be universal, but its legal and tax implications are not.*

Even among physically replicated funds, nuances abound. Some ETFs reinvest dividends automatically; others distribute them periodically. Some use in-kind creation and redemption, which minimises capital gains distributions and enhances tax efficiency. Others settle in cash, exposing shareholders to taxable events. These structural levers are largely invisible to the casual investor, yet they materially shape outcomes. An ETF that avoids triggering capital gains for two decades is a different beast than one that quietly builds a tax burden along the way. *It is not enough to know what an ETF holds—you must understand how it holds it.*

Issuer quality adds yet another layer of complexity. The ETF boom has attracted a wide range of providers—from venerable institutions with deep trading desks and compliance infrastructure to newer entrants whose chief innovation is marketing flair. While competition has been broadly beneficial for investors, it has also led to a proliferation of ETFs designed less for investor outcomes and more for asset gathering. This distinction matters. Reputable issuers invest in index tracking precision, risk controls, and fund governance. They also have a track record of closing underperforming or illiquid funds in an orderly fashion, with clear shareholder communication. Lesser-known providers may be quicker to chase fads, slower to address tracking issues, and less transparent about fund operations. *Past issuer behaviour is one of the most reliable predictors of future investor experience.*

None of this is to say that newer or smaller ETF providers are inherently inferior. Some offer niche exposures or innovative structures that large incumbents have ignored. But differentiation must be rooted in execution, not just narrative. An ETF promising "next-generation AI disruption" may sound exciting, but if it charges a 1.2% expense ratio, rebalances erratically, and holds 40% cash for liquidity, then it's more marketing vehicle than investment product. The same applies to core index funds. A low headline fee is irrelevant if tracking error wipes out the cost advantage. Investors must learn to ask: *Is this ETF doing what it claims to do—and doing it well?*

Due diligence begins with transparency. Fortunately, most reputable ETFs publish detailed data about holdings, tracking performance, rebalancing schedules, and fee structures. These disclosures are not just regulatory obligations—they're decision-making tools. But using them requires effort. Reading a factsheet is not analysis. True scrutiny involves looking at historical performance versus benchmark, analysing deviation during periods of market stress, and examining how consistently the fund maintains exposure. It also involves reviewing bid-ask spreads, daily trading volume, and creation/redemption activity—all of which provide insight into liquidity and execution risk. *A fund that trades at a tight spread during volatile markets signals robustness. One that goes quiet or deviates sharply from NAV demands caution.*

Investors should also examine securities lending policies. Some ETF issuers lend out underlying assets to generate additional income, which is often shared with shareholders. This can enhance returns slightly, especially for large funds with high-quality collateral. But lending practices vary in transparency, risk management, and revenue sharing. Some providers return nearly all proceeds to shareholders; others keep a disproportionate share. Understanding the fund's lending approach—and its associated risk disclosures—adds another layer to the selection process. It's not just about whether lending occurs, but how well it is governed. *The devil is in the disclosure.*

A further distinction worth noting is fund closure risk. Thousands of ETFs have launched over the past two decades—but not all have survived. Low-volume or narrowly focused ETFs are more likely to be shut down, often with little warning. While shareholders usually receive the fund's net asset value upon liquidation, the process can trigger unintended taxes, bid-ask spread losses, and strategic disruption. Investors chasing niche exposure without considering fund sustainability may find themselves forced to sell at a bad time. Avoiding this scenario means considering not only the fund's current popularity, but its long-term viability, sponsor commitment, and competitive positioning.

All of this may seem daunting at first. But the takeaway is simple: the ETF market demands more than passive acceptance. It demands active awareness. Selecting an ETF should not feel like ordering from a takeaway menu. It should feel like assembling machinery—machinery that will power your wealth over decades. Precision matters. Engineering matters. And durability matters more than design. *You do not need to be an ETF technician—but you do need to think like one.*

Ultimately, this is about responsibility. When you invest through ETFs, you are outsourcing decisions—replication, rebalancing, tax strategy—to a fund structure and an issuer. That delegation can be powerful, but only if the system you delegate to is trustworthy, efficient, and aligned with your interests. The superficial similarities between funds lull many investors into indifference. But indifference compounds into mediocrity. Discernment compounds into confidence. The more thoughtfully you understand what you're buying, the less likely you are to react impulsively, abandon your plan, or chase the latest product.

Look past the label. Lift the hood. Because in ETF investing, the beauty is not in the branding—it's in the build.

Volume, Liquidity, and the Mirage of Popularity

Not all popularity is productive. In the investment world, this truth is often obscured by the allure of large numbers. Assets under management (AUM) are frequently used as a shorthand for credibility, quality, or safety. The logic appears sound: if billions of pounds are flowing into a fund, surely it must be doing something right. But the reality is more complex—and, at times, counterintuitive. Size alone does not equal strength, and high trading volume does not always signal functional liquidity. In fact, relying too heavily on these metrics can lead investors into a false sense of security—overlooking structural weaknesses, ignoring real costs, and missing superior alternatives cloaked in modest volume.

Understanding volume and liquidity—where they overlap, where they diverge, and where they mislead—is essential for any serious ETF investor. The distinction between apparent popularity and true investability can be subtle, but mastering it brings clarity to decision-making and confidence in execution. ETFs are often marketed through numbers: lowest fees, highest AUM, most traded. Yet the metrics that matter most are not always the ones splashed across a factsheet.

Let's begin with volume, a metric widely misunderstood. Daily trading volume tells us how many shares of an ETF change hands in a typical session. It is a measure of activity, not accessibility. An ETF that trades heavily may be easy to buy or sell in large quantities without affecting its price. But volume itself is backward-looking—it reflects interest, not quality. More critically, volume does not determine liquidity in the way most investors assume. This is a foundational misconception that deserves to be corrected.

ETF liquidity is a function of two intertwined markets: the primary and the secondary. In the secondary market—what retail investors see on their screens—ETFs trade like shares. Bids and offers form a visible order book, and volume data gives a rough sense of how often the fund is bought and sold. But underneath this sits the primary market, where large institutional players—known as authorised participants (APs)—create or redeem ETF shares by delivering or receiving the underlying assets. This structural feature means that ETF liquidity is not strictly tied to the volume of ETF units changing hands. *What matters more is the liquidity of the underlying securities.*

For instance, an ETF that tracks the FTSE 100 can scale effortlessly, even if its own trading volume appears low. The APs can readily create or redeem shares because the FTSE 100 itself is a liquid, well-traded universe. Conversely, an ETF tracking a frontier market index may exhibit high ETF trading volume, but suffer from real illiquidity if the underlying stocks are thinly traded or subject to capital controls. *Apparent ETF liquidity is only as strong as the liquidity of its underlying holdings.*

Bid-ask spreads offer a more precise lens. A tight spread—say, a penny or two wide—generally indicates strong liquidity and healthy competition among market makers. Wider spreads, particularly during volatile markets, can result in immediate costs to investors, especially those trading frequently or with large orders. These costs are often underestimated. A 0.3% spread might seem trivial, but it can easily exceed an ETF's annual expense ratio in a single transaction. *Ignoring trading costs while obsessing over annual fees is a common, costly error.*

This is where the mirage of popularity takes hold. A fund with enormous AUM may still carry wide spreads if market maker competition is low, or if trading is dominated by institutional block orders away from the public book. On the other hand, a smaller ETF with moderate volume may still be highly liquid if its market makers are efficient and the underlying assets are easy to source. *Liquidity is engineered, not inherited.* Investors need to assess it with the same rigour they apply to asset allocation or fee analysis.

Take, for example, two ETFs tracking the same corporate bond index. One has £10 billion in AUM and trades 3 million shares a day; the other has £500 million and trades a few hundred thousand. At first glance, the former seems superior. But if the smaller fund has a tighter spread, more consistent NAV pricing, and a longer history of precise index tracking, it may actually be the more investable choice. Conversely, the larger fund's apparent liquidity could be distorted by a few large players executing off-book trades that mask true retail access. *Popularity does not guarantee performance—and certainly not efficiency.*

There is also the question of crowding. High AUM in a narrow strategy can create problems of its own. When too much money chases a limited set of assets, distortions occur. Bid-ask spreads widen, rebalancing becomes harder, and index tracking may deteriorate. In extreme cases, the ETF itself begins to influence the price of its constituents—a perverse inversion of passive investing. This is especially true in small-cap, high-yield, or niche thematic

ETFs, where inflows can overwhelm the underlying market. *A fund can be too successful for its own good.*

The paradox of ETF scale is that it invites complacency. Investors assume that large, popular funds are de facto better—more liquid, more efficient, more robust. But history offers cautionary tales. The collapse of highly traded leveraged ETFs during market shocks. The closure of mega-AUM thematic funds after sudden outflows. The reclassification of popular China ETFs following regulatory shifts. In each case, popularity masked fragility. *What everyone owns is not necessarily what everyone should own.*

That said, size and volume are not meaningless. For institutional investors executing large block trades, high volume may reduce execution risk. For tactical traders, narrow spreads matter more than tracking error. For long-term holders, high AUM can offer comfort that the fund is unlikely to be shut down. But even here, nuance matters. A fund's survivability is influenced not only by its size, but by the issuer's strategic priorities. Niche funds with moderate AUM may still be retained if they serve a strategic purpose or reinforce a brand. *Quantitative thresholds are always interpreted within qualitative context.*

Retail investors in particular need to recalibrate their instincts. Buying the most popular fund is not due diligence. Nor is it a substitute for understanding how the ETF operates. Liquidity is dynamic—it expands in calm markets and vanishes in stress. Volume can be gamed. AUM can rise from hype. None of these attributes tell you whether a fund will do what it claims, when it matters most. *The test of an ETF is not its statistics, but its structure.*

A better approach is triangulation. Evaluate the fund's spread history over different market conditions. Review how closely it tracks its index over months and years, not just days. Assess whether the volume comes from a diverse investor base or is dominated by a few large trades. Look at creation-redemption activity, which reveals how readily APs can manage supply and demand. These are the fingerprints of true liquidity—and they require active inspection, not passive acceptance.

In sum, volume and AUM are signals, not guarantees. Popularity is not a proxy for precision. Investors must resist the temptation to equate big with better and busy with safe. ETFs are financial technology, and like all technologies, their effectiveness depends on design, context, and maintenance. *Choose your tools not because they are familiar, but because they are fit for purpose.*

Liquidity is a dynamic property. It is not inherent in the ticker, but in the interplay between market makers, APs, underlying assets, and investor behaviour. Understanding this complexity isn't optional—it is central to intelligent ETF selection. Because in investing, what's easy to buy isn't always worth owning. And what's widely held isn't always wisely held.

Beware the Niche Trap

Excitement is easy to manufacture in the world of finance. All it takes is a captivating theme, a slick ticker symbol, and a promise of exposure to the "next big thing." Niche and thematic ETFs thrive in this atmosphere. They offer specificity with seductive narratives—cybersecurity, cannabis, blockchain, space exploration, clean water, pet care, even Millennial spending habits. For investors hungry for meaning or novelty, they appear to offer precision and relevance. But this precision often masks a profound weakness: *the illusion of diversification.* Under the bonnet, many of these ETFs are little more than marketing constructs stitched together with loosely correlated assets, fragile liquidity, and disproportionate exposure to a handful of names.

Thematic investing is not new. Sector rotation strategies have long existed, and so have narrowly focused funds. But the explosion of niche ETFs in the past decade is different. What used to require institutional resources and sector-specific analysis is now available with a click and a story. Today's thematic ETFs are consumer products as much as financial instruments—built less to optimise long-term returns than to capitalise on behavioural triggers. The framing is psychological: thematic ETFs tap into identity, aspiration, and narrative, rather than asset class or market structure. The result is that investors are often buying *ideas*, not strategies. This can be empowering—or profoundly misleading.

A critical issue is concentration. Many thematic ETFs boast exposure to 30, 40, or 50 companies, yet their effective diversification is far narrower. A top-heavy weighting—where the top five holdings represent 40% or more of the total portfolio—is common. These funds may claim to offer access to an entire "theme," but in practice they hinge on the fate of a small group of high-beta stocks. If these underperform, the entire ETF suffers, regardless of how the broader theme plays out. *The narrative may be diversified; the returns are not.*

Consider the example of the cannabis sector. When ETFs focusing on marijuana stocks gained attention in 2018, they surged on speculation, policy momentum, and investor enthusiasm. But most of these funds were concentrated in a few unprofitable Canadian growers with fragile balance sheets and inconsistent regulatory footing. As fundamentals failed to meet hype, and oversupply met tepid demand, valuations collapsed. Investors who had bought the "theme" were stuck with the reality: poor governance, weak earnings, and regulatory headwinds. The ETF wrapper could not protect against bad companies or bad timing. *A theme cannot substitute for due diligence.*

This pattern recurs across thematic products. Whether it's artificial intelligence, ESG-friendly innovation, or climate tech, investors must ask: is this fund investing in the theme directly, or merely in companies adjacent to it? Often, the underlying holdings are a patchwork of tangential relationships—firms that may benefit marginally from the theme, but whose core business lies elsewhere. A "blockchain ETF" might include semiconductors, exchanges, and financials with only passing relevance to decentralised ledgers. A "cybersecurity ETF" may hold large-cap tech companies that derive only a fraction of their revenue from security solutions. *The packaging does not guarantee purity.*

Liquidity and scalability pose additional concerns. Thematic ETFs tend to focus on small- or mid-cap stocks, many of which trade thinly and can be difficult to price during stress. As assets under management grow, ETF flows can distort the valuations of these smaller companies, creating artificial demand and inflating prices beyond fundamental value. When inflows reverse or enthusiasm fades, the resulting unwind can be sharp and unforgiving. For investors, this means not just poor performance, but poor execution—slippage, wide spreads, and tracking errors that erode value quietly but consistently. *Novelty has a cost, and it is rarely listed in the factsheet.*

There is also the risk of redundancy. Many thematic ETFs have substantial overlap with broad-based sector funds or even core equity indexes. A "future mobility ETF" may hold Tesla, Alphabet, Apple, and Nvidia—companies already present in a global equity fund or a technology index. Investors may believe they are diversifying, when in fact they are doubling down on the same risk factors. *The appearance of thematic diversification can conceal portfolio concentration.*

Timing, too, is a subtle trap. The launch of many niche ETFs coincides with peak optimism around a theme. By the time a product becomes available for public investment, the underlying idea may already be priced in. This leads to a well-documented "ETF performance gap," where new thematic funds often underperform their stated benchmarks within 12–24 months of launch. Investors enter late, stay too long, and exit after the narrative has decayed. The irony is painful: the very structure designed to make investing more accessible can magnify behavioural mistakes. *Access does not equal advantage.*

That said, not all specificity is dangerous. There are legitimate cases where a thematic ETF offers useful exposure—particularly in portfolios seeking satellite positions or tactical tilts. A carefully constructed climate transition ETF, for example, may complement a broader ESG strategy if it is backed by robust index methodology, transparent screening criteria, and sensible diversification. Similarly, funds that focus on essential infrastructure or demographic trends may provide long-term relevance if they are rooted in solid fundamentals. The distinction lies in construction, not just concept. *Useful specificity is engineered; hype is assembled.*

To navigate the niche trap, investors need to move from storytelling to scrutiny. Begin with the index: who designed it, what are the inclusion criteria, how often is it rebalanced? Examine the weightings: are they equal, market cap-based, or tilted toward volatility? Look at the holdings: how many are truly aligned with the theme, and how many are passengers? Evaluate liquidity: will this fund remain viable in a downturn, or will it shrink into irrelevance? These are not aesthetic questions; they are structural ones. *A compelling idea must be matched by a credible vehicle.*

It's also worth considering psychological fit. Thematic ETFs can be emotionally volatile, rising and falling with headlines, hype cycles, and investor sentiment. For long-term investors who value stability, this can undermine discipline and confidence. If a fund is exciting enough to make you check your portfolio weekly, it may not be the right fit—no matter how noble the narrative. *Sustainability in investing means emotional, not just environmental, alignment.*

There is nothing inherently wrong with investing in ideas. Innovation should be celebrated. But the question is not whether a theme is compelling—it's whether the ETF that claims to represent it is structured to endure. This is the core distinction between marketing and mechanism. *An ETF is not a belief system; it is a financial instrument. And instruments must be judged by how they perform, not how they sound.*

The rise of thematic ETFs reflects a broader truth about modern investing: access is no longer the primary problem. Selection is. With hundreds of niche products competing for attention, the challenge is not choosing what's interesting—it's choosing what's resilient. When everyone is offering a story, wisdom lies in demanding structure. What's rare is not the next big theme, but the discipline to ask whether the vehicle matches the vision.

Because in the end, performance is not delivered by ideas alone—it is delivered by design.

The Three-Bucket Test

Good portfolio design is not a matter of finding the best ETF—it's a matter of understanding how each ETF fits. The real challenge is not selection, but composition: knowing how to assemble different exposures into a structure that reflects both financial logic and psychological sustainability. That's where the three-bucket model becomes indispensable. By classifying ETFs as *Core*, *Satellite*, or *Speculative*, investors can shift from impulsive allocation to intentional design. This framework is not a gimmick. It is a disciplined method for managing complexity, reducing cognitive noise, and anchoring decisions to purpose rather than emotion.

Start with the Core. These ETFs form the bedrock of your portfolio. They are broad, well-diversified, low-cost funds designed to capture long-term market growth across geographies, sectors, and capitalisations. A global equity index tracker, a total bond market ETF, or a world-allocation fund fits this category. The Core is not exciting, and it's not meant to be. Its job is to compound steadily, quietly, and predictably. Investors often undervalue Core holdings because they don't generate headlines or dramatic returns in a short time. But over decades, it is the Core that determines the outcome. *Performance is not driven by brilliance at the edges, but by strength at the centre.*

The Satellite bucket supports and supplements the Core. These ETFs express strategic tilts or intentional overweights—perhaps in emerging markets, small caps, real estate, or specific sectors like healthcare or clean energy. Unlike the Core, Satellite positions are selective by design. They allow investors to incorporate views, convictions, or underrepresented exposures without disrupting overall balance. Crucially, Satellite ETFs should be diversified enough to withstand shocks, but targeted enough to add differentiation. This is where analytical thinking meets portfolio nuance. *The Satellite is not a playground for hunches—it's a tool for precision.*

Then there's the Speculative bucket—where risk meets restraint. These ETFs are high-conviction, high-volatility positions that represent asymmetric bets or thematic exposure: cryptocurrency infrastructure, frontier tech, leveraged strategies, or narrow thematic plays like space exploration or genomics. Their role is not to anchor the portfolio but to add optionality. By isolating these positions within a clearly defined bucket, investors can engage curiosity and optimism without letting those impulses dominate the overall strategy. The point is not to eliminate risk but to *contain* it. *Speculation, when bounded, can be constructive. When it bleeds into the Core, it becomes corrosive.*

This three-bucket structure achieves two things simultaneously: clarity and discipline. It clarifies the *function* of each ETF, transforming the portfolio from a collection of products into a coherent system. And it imposes *discipline* on allocation decisions. For example, if a fund is clearly speculative—volatile, narrative-driven, and undiversified—it has no business occupying more than a small percentage of your total assets. Conversely, if a fund is truly Core-worthy, it should not be dismissed or underweighted simply because it's dull. *The structure enforces alignment between purpose and position size.*

A practical benefit of the three-bucket model is emotional containment. Volatility feels different when it's happening where you expect it. A thematic ETF falling 30% is tolerable—if it sits in the Speculative bucket with 5% exposure. The same loss is psychologically destructive if that ETF was mistaken for a Core holding. Similarly, watching Core ETFs deliver average returns is reassuring when you recognise their function is stability, not excitement. *Mismatched expectations are the root of portfolio regret.*

Misclassification is common and costly. Many investors mistake Satellite ETFs for Core positions, overloading on regional or sector-specific funds while believing they are broadly diversified. Others elevate speculative funds into central positions simply because they are trending or high-performing. This leads to overexposure, excessive drawdowns, and eventually, a panicked flight from risk—often at the worst time. The three-bucket test forces re-evaluation. Ask: *What role is this ETF playing, and is it suited for that role?* Form must match function.

Critics might argue that this framework oversimplifies the complexity of portfolio design. But its value lies precisely in its simplicity. Asset management professionals already use variations of this structure, often referred to as core-satellite strategies, to ensure that decisions scale well and remain coherent as portfolios evolve. What the three-bucket model offers is accessibility without dilution.

It's a portable mental model that works whether you're managing £10,000 or £10 million. *Sophistication is not the same as complication.*

The model also fosters intellectual humility. It accepts that investors will be tempted by trends, stories, and high-risk opportunities. Rather than pretending these impulses don't exist, it gives them a place—quarantined, quantified, and proportioned. This is not cynicism; it's design. Just as a well-built city allocates space for industry, parks, and housing, a well-built portfolio allows for growth, exploration, and safety—each in their own domain. *Discipline is not denial; it is architecture.*

When applied correctly, the three-bucket test also improves communication—especially for advisors, families, and partners managing wealth together. Explaining an allocation decision becomes easier when you can say: "This fund is Core because it's globally diversified and cost-efficient," or "This is a Speculative position, so we're keeping it under 3%." It changes the tone of investing conversations from anecdotal to strategic, and from reactive to intentional. *Language structures thought, and thought structures behaviour.*

Over time, investors can evolve the balance between buckets as their life stage, risk tolerance, and market outlook change. Younger investors might skew heavier toward Satellite and even modest Speculative exposure, given longer time horizons and a capacity for volatility. Retirees, in contrast, might concentrate on the Core, prioritising stability and predictable income. But regardless of allocation, the framework remains consistent. *What matters is not how the buckets are filled, but that they exist and are distinct.*

There is one final advantage: behavioural insulation. Markets will tempt, panic, and confuse. But a portfolio built on clearly delineated roles provides psychological anchors. When headlines scream about the "next big opportunity," you know it belongs—if at all—in the Speculative corner. When markets crash and even the Core falls, you know not to sell the foundation to fix the ceiling. When Satellite strategies lag, you understand they're designed to complement, not replace. *The buckets act not just as categories, but as commitments.*

The ETF universe is large, fluid, and increasingly crowded. Without a conceptual map, the sheer volume of choice can overwhelm even experienced investors. The three-bucket test is that map. It restores order by mapping function to form, allocation to intention, and exposure to expectation. It removes the illusion that every ETF deserves equal attention or equal weight. And most importantly, it gives investors the one thing that can't be bought in a product: *clarity of purpose.*

The strongest portfolios aren't built from conviction alone—they are built from structure. And structure begins with knowing not just what you hold, but *why* you hold it—and where it belongs.

Chapter 5
The Family of Funds — Understanding ETF Archetypes

No serious investor can afford to treat ETFs as interchangeable. Beneath their similar tickers and digital polish lies a sophisticated taxonomy of structure, strategy, and purpose. To invest intelligently in ETFs is to recognise that each fund serves a distinct role, behaves differently under stress, and carries its own spectrum of risk. This chapter is concerned with pattern recognition—not of fleeting market trends, but of fund design itself. It's about identifying archetypes within the ETF universe, so that selection is guided by function and fit rather than by excitement or branding. Classification fosters clarity; clarity fosters conviction.

The modern ETF landscape feels democratic—every fund a click away, every index seemingly accessible. Yet access is not understanding. The central question today is rarely whether you *can* buy exposure to something, but whether you *should*. Distinguishing a total market tracker from a thematic sector play, or a short-duration bond ETF from a leveraged emerging-market instrument, is more than an academic exercise. It is a survival skill. The future trajectory of your portfolio depends less on what you own and more on whether each holding fits into a reasoned system.

We begin with foundational instruments: broad index ETFs. These are not merely passive products—they are philosophical commitments. Owning a total market or S&P 500 fund is a vote for discipline over prediction, breadth over brilliance. Market returns are delivered unapologetically: average in the short term, profoundly compounding in the long. These funds do not chase alpha; they accumulate quietly. Investors who grasp this distinction will not abandon them when panic spreads.

Stability, however, is only half the story. Markets are mosaics of narratives, and ETFs increasingly serve as vehicles to express those narratives. Sector and thematic ETFs allow investors to lean into conviction—healthcare innovation, green energy, artificial intelligence, infrastructure. Used judiciously, they are precision tools capturing structural shifts or hedging vulnerabilities. Used recklessly, they become speculation masquerading as diversification. This section explores evaluation beyond names: the number of holdings, correlation with broader markets, and sensitivity to macroeconomic shocks. Conviction must be earned, not marketed.

Bond ETFs introduce subtler complexities. Often misperceived as inherently "safe," fixed-income funds are highly sensitive to interest rates, credit spreads, inflation expectations, and policy shifts. They serve as ballast, but ballast is not immunity. Choosing the right bond ETF requires trade-offs: yield versus duration, domestic versus global exposure, investment-grade versus high-yield credit. Here, we learn to peer inside the wrapper and avoid the false security of the label "bond fund." Risk in fixed income is nuanced—and therefore easily underestimated.

Globalisation adds another layer. Exposure to international and emerging markets is alluring—and increasingly essential. Yet it demands more than geographic curiosity: currency risk, political stability, liquidity, corporate governance—all factor in. ETFs tracking emerging economies are not mere plays on growth; they intertwine exposure to fragility and dynamism. This section explores how to access global markets intelligently, avoiding over-concentration and recognising when a regional fund is proxying for other risks—commodities, currency, or geopolitical uncertainty.

Each ETF type tells a story—not merely about what it tracks, but how it should be used. Understanding this family empowers allocation decisions rooted in foresight rather than fashion, defending against portfolios built from headlines, peer comparisons, or short-term performance tables. The seasoned investor sees beyond the label, past the marketing, into the structural DNA of each fund.

Tensions and trade-offs emerge naturally. Thematic ETFs offer specificity, but often at the cost of diversification. Total market ETFs provide neutrality, yet this can suppress legitimate conviction. A thoughtful portfolio balances breadth and focus, safety and expression, anchored in the understanding of what each fund was built to do—and what it was not.

The ETF is not a single instrument—it is a toolbox. Misuse arises when one attempts to wield the wrong tool for the wrong task: a scalpel to drive nails, a sledgehammer to carve fine detail. Categorisation is essential; education, not enthusiasm, prevents error. By the end of this chapter, the reader will recognise the principal ETF archetypes and understand how to deploy them responsibly, proportionally, and purposefully.

This is not about memorising fund names. It is about constructing a mental latticework: a framework for slotting each fund into a known structure, assessing its role, and judging its fit. The most effective investors are not those who know the most tickers—they are those who know where each exposure belongs, and why.

Ultimately, understanding ETF types is a safeguard against confusion, misallocation, and regret. It empowers the investor to resist complexity for its own sake, to reject performance-chasing, and to select funds that serve, rather than merely excite. ETF selection thus becomes an act of design rather than reaction. From design comes coherence; from coherence, resilience; and from resilience, long-term success.

Index Funds: The Purest Form of Discipline

Every serious conversation about investing eventually returns to one quiet truth: most people would be far better off owning the market than trying to beat it. Index funds—particularly total market and S&P 500 ETFs—embody that truth with elegant simplicity. They do not promise excitement. They promise exposure. They do not chase alpha. They capture the beta of capitalism itself. And they do so with an efficiency, transparency, and discipline that most active strategies only approximate in theory, not in practice.

The appeal of indexing is not its complexity, but its *resistance to it.* In a financial world awash with overconfidence, noise, and over-engineered products, index funds are a refuge of restraint. They remind the investor that compounding does not require cleverness—only consistency. The decision to invest in a total market ETF or an S&P 500 fund is not a passive one. It is *an active choice to opt out of illusion.* It is the investor's way of saying: "I do not need to outperform everyone. I need to own everything—and let time do its work."

At the heart of this discipline is the concept of *broad participation.* A total market ETF—such as those tracking the CRSP US Total Market Index or the Russell 3000—holds thousands of equities across sectors and market capitalisations. It is not making a bet on which company will succeed; it is placing a wager that *the system itself will keep producing winners.* An S&P 500 ETF narrows the lens slightly, focusing on large-cap companies that represent roughly 80% of the U.S. equity market. Yet even in its narrower scope, it is diversified across industries and companies that reflect the beating heart of the American economy.

What makes these funds powerful is not their components alone, but *the discipline they enforce on the investor.* There is no room for tinkering. There is no rotation, no subjective calls on what to overweight or underweight. Index ETFs rebalance automatically to reflect the index, not the investor's moods. That mechanical fidelity is not a bug. It is the feature. *Left alone, these instruments will do their job. The question is whether the investor will.*

The data behind indexing is no longer controversial. Decades of academic research and market evidence show that most actively managed funds underperform their benchmark over time, especially after accounting for fees and taxes. The idea that an investor could consistently pick superior managers or time their entry and exit to outperform a low-cost index ETF has been tested—and found wanting. This is not a criticism of skill. It is an acknowledgement of probability. *The edge that matters is not intellectual. It's behavioural.*

Index ETFs offer more than cost savings. They offer *a framework for staying invested through volatility.* When the market drops 10%, the index investor does not ask, "Which fund manager should I fire?" They know what they own: a slice of every listed company in the index. There is no second-guessing the strategy, because the strategy is structural. This removes a key psychological trap: the temptation to intervene at precisely the wrong time. A well-constructed index ETF is not just a product. It is *a psychological buffer* against panic.

Critics of indexing often argue that it is "average." That critique misunderstands the point entirely. The average of a well-functioning market is *extraordinary*—especially when compounded over decades. The S&P 500, for instance, has delivered long-term annual returns of roughly 8–10% historically, even through recessions, wars, pandemics, and political upheaval. Owning the index means owning that resilience. And doing so at a cost measured in basis points, not percentages.

Another objection suggests that indexing leads to market distortions—that too much capital flowing passively into the same securities creates pricing inefficiencies or bubbles. This concern is not trivial, but it is often overstated. Index ETFs do not dictate price; they *follow market cap*, meaning their weights are driven by price movements in the underlying securities, not the other way around. Moreover, the presence of passive capital does not eliminate the role of active investors. Markets still respond to earnings, news, and expectations because *there is always someone trading actively*. Indexing does not extinguish price discovery. It simply allows more investors to benefit from it without trying to outsmart it.

Perhaps the most underappreciated feature of index ETFs is their role in global portfolio design. A U.S.-based investor may begin with a domestic total market fund, but can easily expand into international developed or emerging markets using similar index vehicles. This allows for *geographic diversification without stylistic inconsistency*. The investor is not switching between philosophies—they are extending the same disciplined approach across borders.

From an implementation standpoint, index ETFs also offer superior tax efficiency. Their unique structure—particularly in the U.S.—allows fund managers to use *in-kind redemptions* to minimise capital gains distributions. For long-term investors, this can translate into meaningful savings. Combined with ultra-low expense ratios—often below 0.05%—the compounding drag is minimal. Over a 30-year horizon, the difference between paying 0.05% and 1.00% annually is not subtle. It is transformative.

But the most powerful argument for indexing may be philosophical. In a world obsessed with immediacy, it asks for patience. In a culture built on hyper-specialisation, it celebrates breadth. In an industry incentivised to sell performance, it sells *process*. It is a radical act of humility—*to say "I do not know which companies will win, but I trust that some will"*. That humility, paradoxically, produces better results than the confidence to constantly predict.

This is not to say index funds are flawless. They are vulnerable to short-term underperformance relative to sectors or styles that surge in a given year. They offer no protection in a bear market—they go down with the market they track. But they do not claim otherwise. *They are not engineered for downside protection. They are engineered for endurance.* Their edge is not in timing, but in staying.

For most investors—particularly those with long horizons, finite time, and no professional edge—index ETFs are not just sufficient. They are optimal. They provide exposure to the collective intelligence of the market, at minimal cost, with structural integrity. They eliminate unnecessary decisions and focus attention on what really matters: contribution rate, time horizon, and staying the course.

An investor who holds a broad index ETF, rebalances periodically, and ignores the noise is not doing nothing. They are executing a strategy more rigorous than most professionals. It is a strategy that reflects the rarest form of intelligence in investing: *the willingness to be bored, disciplined, and right over time.*

To own an index ETF is to own a philosophy of patience in a marketplace of urgency. It is not the absence of a plan. It is the highest form of one.

Sector and Thematic Funds: High-Conviction Tools

For the long-term investor, the allure of simplicity and breadth often finds its home in broad index ETFs. But there comes a point when nuance becomes necessary—when a portfolio must speak not only to markets as a whole, but to *what the investor believes* about change, innovation, or risk. Sector and thematic funds exist in this space. They are not substitutes for diversification. They are expressions of conviction—targeted tools that allow an investor to tilt their exposure toward specific economic trends, industries, or structural shifts. Used judiciously, they can complement a disciplined core. Used carelessly, they can unravel it.

At their most basic level, sector ETFs offer concentrated exposure to defined segments of the economy—technology, healthcare, energy, financials, consumer staples, and so on. These funds typically mirror the sector breakdowns defined by classification systems like GICS (Global Industry Classification Standard) and are often derived from broader benchmarks like the S&P 500. A technology sector ETF, for instance, might include Apple, Microsoft, and Nvidia, while excluding companies in unrelated industries. The appeal is intuitive: if you believe a particular sector is poised for outperformance, a sector ETF allows you to express that view with precision.

But precision comes with trade-offs. By narrowing the lens, the investor accepts greater volatility and concentration risk. Technology, for example, may drive returns in one decade and drag them in the next. Sector leadership is inherently cyclical. Healthcare might shine in defensive periods, while energy booms and busts with commodity prices and global demand. The investor who builds a portfolio solely around these moving targets is not allocating—they are gambling. The challenge is not that sector funds are flawed, but that their clarity of purpose can tempt overuse. *The tool is not dangerous. Misuse is.*

Thematic ETFs are even more targeted—and often more speculative. Unlike sector funds, which track established industries, thematic funds aim to capture emerging trends: artificial intelligence, blockchain, renewable energy, genomics, space exploration, and so forth. These funds tend to cross sector boundaries, bundling companies based on a narrative rather than a traditional economic role. A clean energy ETF, for example, may include utility companies, industrial firms, tech startups, and rare earth miners—entities that might have little in common outside of the chosen story. This flexibility is both their strength and their liability.

Thematic ETFs appeal to a very human desire: *the wish to be early*. To capture the wave before it crests. Yet this desire can obscure critical questions. Is the theme investable, or merely aspirational? Are the companies inside the fund actually profitable, or just correlated with a marketing trend? What are the weighting mechanisms, the rebalancing rules, the turnover costs? Does the theme have staying power—or is it merely the product of short-term excitement? These are not semantic concerns. They go to the heart of whether a thematic ETF is a sound investment or a disguised lottery ticket.

Another challenge is the issue of crowding. When a thematic ETF becomes popular—especially on social media or among retail trading platforms—it can experience rapid inflows that distort its price relative to the underlying fundamentals. This popularity is self-reinforcing until it isn't. Investors who enter late often discover that *they were not investing in a theme—they were subsidising someone else's exit.* The line between innovation and speculation is not always visible in advance, but hindsight makes it painfully clear.

Still, to dismiss sector and thematic ETFs entirely would be to throw away an important part of the toolkit. The key is integration. These funds work best not as the main engine, but as satellite positions—complementing a diversified core that anchors the portfolio across cycles. A thoughtful investor might allocate 80–90% to broad-based index funds and reserve the remainder for targeted tilts that reflect personal insight or strategic hedges. For example, an investor working in biotech may allocate a small percentage to a healthcare innovation ETF—not because they expect immediate alpha, but because they understand the field deeply and want their portfolio to reflect that conviction.

In other cases, sector funds can function defensively. Utilities and consumer staples may offer ballast in a downturn. Financials may benefit from rising interest rates. Energy can hedge inflationary spikes. These are not bold bets—they are strategic overlays that allow the investor to *position around macro conditions* without abandoning a diversified base.

This underscores a larger point: sector and thematic ETFs require not just knowledge, but *self-awareness*. Why do you believe in this sector or theme? What evidence supports that belief? What is your time horizon? How will you behave if the position underperforms for two or three years? If the answer is discomfort, over-allocation, or panic-selling, the position is too large. A good rule of thumb: your thematic tilt should be small enough to fail without derailing your long-term plan. If the core is the house, the sector fund is the room. If the core is the engine, the thematic fund is the trim. *They are allowed to be exciting—but they must remain optional.*

From a cost and structure perspective, these ETFs vary widely. Some are managed passively against a custom index; others are actively managed in disguise. Expense ratios can be significantly higher than for broad index funds, often ranging from 0.3% to over 0.7%. Liquidity may be lower. Underlying holdings may be thinly traded. Turnover is often higher, introducing more tax drag. Investors must scrutinise the methodology, the tracking error, the issuer's transparency, and the fund's actual holdings—not just its name. *The wrapper may say "space economy," but the contents could be a handful of satellite telecom firms and speculative defence contractors.* Know what you own.

Timing also matters. Many thematic ETFs are launched at or near the peak of public interest in the theme. This is not coincidental. Issuers are incentivised to capitalise on demand. The result is often a painful cycle: fund launches, gains attention, attracts inflows, disappoints, and fades. The shelf life of many thematic ETFs is short. Some are closed or merged within a few years. Survivorship bias distorts the historical data. Investors remember the winners but forget the graveyard of failed ideas.

Yet, despite the risks, these funds have a place—when used with discipline. They allow investors to express views in a transparent, diversified, and liquid format. They replace the need to pick single stocks. They can serve as tools for learning, for hedging, for aligning values with capital (e.g., ESG themes), or for tilting toward perceived structural change. The problem is not the funds. It is the tendency to *confuse conviction with certainty*.

The wise use of sector and thematic ETFs begins with a question: *What am I trying to solve for?* If the answer is boredom, the product is probably a mistake. If the answer is targeted exposure within a thoughtful portfolio, the product may be fit for purpose. The ETF structure remains robust—it is the intent behind it that determines its utility.

Ultimately, every investor must decide how much voice they want to give to their predictions. Broad index funds whisper: "You don't need to know everything. Just own everything." Sector and thematic funds reply: "You know *something*. Use it wisely." Between these voices lies the opportunity for balance—and the responsibility to manage it.

Bond ETFs: Stability You Can Count On—Sometimes

There is a persistent myth in personal finance that bonds are the grown-up corner of the investment world—steady, reliable, low drama. For many investors, especially those schooled in traditional asset allocation, bonds are assumed to be the ballast: the predictable counterweight to equity risk, offering income, capital preservation, and a cushion during market stress. But while the asset class as a whole may deserve its reputation for stability, bond ETFs require more scrutiny. They are not bonds; they are portfolios of bonds—and that structural difference matters.

To begin with, bond ETFs trade on exchanges like equities, with live pricing throughout the day. Unlike individual bonds, which have fixed maturity dates and return principal if held to term, bond ETFs are perpetual vehicles. They don't mature. Their holdings roll forward, selling bonds that are nearing expiry and replacing them with new issues to maintain a consistent average duration. That makes them more liquid—but also more exposed to price risk, especially when interest rates shift sharply. *What feels like a static income asset may in fact be dynamically volatile.*

Duration is a concept that demands clear understanding. In essence, it measures a bond's sensitivity to changes in interest rates. A bond ETF with a duration of 5 will fall approximately 5% in price for every 1% rise in interest rates, all else equal. In a falling-rate environment, that sensitivity becomes a tailwind. But when central banks tighten policy, or inflation expectations surge, bond ETFs with long durations can post returns that look more equity-like—in the worst way. Investors who thought they were seeking shelter may find themselves exposed to a different kind of storm.

Consider 2022, when global central banks responded to rising inflation with aggressive rate hikes. Long-dated government bond ETFs in the US, UK, and Europe suffered double-digit losses. For many retail investors, this was their first experience of negative returns from the so-called safe side of the portfolio. The pain wasn't just theoretical. For those nearing retirement or drawing income, the erosion of bond value at the very moment they were relying on it was both financially and psychologically destabilising. *The belief that bonds always buffer equities failed precisely when belief was most needed.*

Credit quality is the second key axis. Bond ETFs span the spectrum from government-backed issues to high-yield, sub-investment-grade debt. The higher the yield, the greater the default risk. This isn't inherently problematic—credit exposure can offer attractive returns in a diversified context. But it does shift the character of the ETF. A high-yield bond fund is not a low-risk diversifier. It behaves more like an equity proxy with income characteristics, often selling off alongside stocks during periods of economic stress. Investors drawn to the "income" of junk bond ETFs must understand they are being compensated for bearing higher default and liquidity risk—not gifted free returns.

One of the more underappreciated aspects of bond ETFs is the role of market-making in keeping them liquid. The bonds themselves often trade in opaque, less liquid over-the-counter markets. But the ETF wrapper benefits from a secondary market, where units can be bought or sold without triggering immediate transactions in the underlying bonds. This keeps spreads relatively tight in normal conditions. However, during periods of market dislocation—as seen in March 2020 during the COVID-driven liquidity crisis—underlying bond markets can freeze, creating pricing disconnects. ETFs may trade at discounts or premiums to their net asset value, undermining the very stability investors sought.

This is where the transparency of bond ETFs comes into focus. While equity ETFs typically hold widely known, publicly listed stocks with observable prices, bond ETFs often contain hundreds or even thousands of securities, many of which do not trade daily. Estimating NAV involves models, approximations, and dealer quotes. It is possible for the ETF's market price to move sharply while the calculated NAV barely shifts, or vice versa. Sophisticated investors understand that the ETF price reflects real-time market sentiment and liquidity—not always the book value of its holdings. But casual investors may mistake price volatility for structural failure, reacting emotionally to moves that are often temporary.

Geographical exposure adds another layer of complexity. Global and emerging market bond ETFs offer diversification away from domestic interest rate cycles, but introduce currency risk, geopolitical instability, and less transparent issuers. Hedged versions exist but add cost and tracking friction. Unhedged versions can deliver unexpected returns—both good and bad—driven more by exchange rate fluctuations than bond performance. Investing in an emerging market bond ETF may sound like accessing high yields in fast-growing economies, but in practice it may mean bearing the risk of capital controls, inflationary spirals, or abrupt devaluations.

None of this means bond ETFs are inappropriate. On the contrary, they remain among the most important innovations in modern portfolio design. They allow investors to access diversified bond exposure without needing large capital outlays or direct access to institutional bond markets. They offer transparency, tax efficiency, and cost competitiveness. But the illusion of simplicity is dangerous. *Bond ETFs are not guaranteed safe harbours. They are tools that demand respect and understanding.*

Choosing the right bond ETF requires aligning three core dimensions: duration, credit, and geography. A short-duration, high-quality government bond ETF is likely to provide stability and liquidity, but low returns. A long-duration corporate bond ETF may offer higher yields, but greater price sensitivity and spread risk. An emerging market bond ETF could deliver diversification, but with higher volatility and political risk. *Each profile suits a different investor need—and none suit all needs at once.*

It is also worth understanding how bond ETFs fit into the broader portfolio construction. If equities are the growth engine, bonds should temper the ride. But this tempering can take different forms. Some investors want their bond allocation to act like cash—stable and available. Others seek income from the bond sleeve, accepting more risk in exchange. Still others use bonds tactically, adjusting duration in response to rate views or macroeconomic forecasts. The ETF universe accommodates all these approaches, but the investor must know their intent. *Confused inputs create confused outcomes.*

There is a philosophical angle to this as well. For decades, the 60/40 portfolio—a mix of 60% equities and 40% bonds—was treated as a near-sacred default for balanced investing. But that assumption was built on decades of declining interest rates and reliable negative correlation between stocks and bonds. When both assets fell together in 2022, the strategy's limitations were laid bare. The experience triggered a wider reconsideration of what role bonds should play—and whether ETF wrappers, however elegant, can compensate for changing economic realities.

This brings us to the final point: context is everything. Bonds may be stabilisers—but only if they're appropriate to the environment and the investor's needs. ETFs may be efficient—but only if the structure aligns with the strategy. Risk may be lower than equities—but it is still risk. What matters is not whether a bond ETF is "good" or "bad," but whether it is *fit for purpose*. And that fitness depends on clarity, intention, and execution.

The disciplined investor asks: *What am I trying to protect? What am I trying to earn? What risks am I absorbing in the process?* The right bond ETF answers those questions without disguise. The wrong one confuses the investor into taking on exposure they do not understand.

Bond ETFs, then, are not safety blankets. They are instruments—finely tuned and context-dependent. They can preserve, protect, or punish. It is the investor's responsibility to understand the mechanics, respect the risks, and ensure that the product fits the plan—not the other way around. Stability is never a given. But with insight and rigour, it can be earned.

Global and Emerging Markets: Investing Without Borders

Most investors are more parochial than they realise. Despite living in a hyperconnected world, where capital flows across borders in milliseconds and information is instantly global, the average investor portfolio remains heavily tilted toward domestic markets. This phenomenon—known as *home bias*—isn't merely a statistical quirk. It is a persistent psychological comfort zone, one that often undermines the very diversification investors claim to seek. Yet stepping beyond that familiarity isn't just a matter of novelty—it's a strategic imperative in modern portfolio design.

Exposure to global and emerging markets through ETFs offers more than access to distant geographies. It opens a window into structural growth stories, demographic tailwinds, and sectoral dynamics unavailable—or underrepresented—in domestic economies. A US-based investor overweight in technology may already have substantial global exposure through multinationals, but that's not the same as owning a fund specifically tracking the MSCI Emerging Markets Index. The nuance lies in intentionality: *Are you global by default, or by design?*

International ETFs vary widely in scope, from broad developed-world funds to country-specific and region-specific offerings. A fund like the iShares MSCI ACWI ex U.S. ETF provides exposure to thousands of companies across developed and emerging economies, from Nestlé and Samsung to Tata Consultancy and MercadoLibre. This breadth allows for a more complete economic representation.

Yet broad does not always mean balanced. Many international indices are disproportionately tilted toward financials, industrials, and commodity sectors, particularly in emerging markets. For the thoughtful investor, this isn't a reason to avoid—but a reason to analyse. *Diversification is not automatic; it must be interrogated.*

Emerging markets, in particular, are a double-edged sword. On one side lies the compelling case: younger populations, rising middle classes, urbanisation, and an expanding role in global trade. On the other lies a thicket of instability: governance risk, weak institutions, capital flight, and currency volatility. ETFs help mitigate some of these risks through diversification and liquidity, but they don't eliminate them. Buying a diversified emerging markets ETF may spread exposure across 20 or more countries, but it doesn't immunise the investor against the effects of a global risk-off sentiment, when money flees all risk assets indiscriminately.

The challenge isn't just country risk. Currency exposure plays a crucial and often underappreciated role in global investing. A British investor buying a US equity ETF unhedged is not just betting on American companies—they are also implicitly betting on the strength of the dollar relative to sterling. That bet can enhance or erode returns, sometimes dramatically. Hedged versions of ETFs exist, but they come with cost and tracking complexity. Worse, they can mute diversification benefits if not carefully chosen. *Currency risk is not noise—it's signal. Understanding it is not optional.*

Geopolitics, too, complicates the calculus. When Russian equities were abruptly removed from global indices following sanctions in 2022, investors learned the hard way that ETF exposure is not immune to capital controls or forced liquidations. In China, the blend of economic promise and political opacity creates an ongoing dilemma: can you benefit from its growth without succumbing to its unpredictability? Many fund providers now offer "ex-China" versions of emerging market ETFs, acknowledging that for some investors, the concentration risk or regulatory discomfort is too great. These are not merely technical decisions; they are expressions of strategy and values.

It's also important to distinguish between emerging and frontier markets. While both are considered developing economies, frontier markets are even less liquid, less regulated, and more volatile. They can offer higher potential upside—but at the cost of significantly greater uncertainty. ETFs focused on these markets tend to have higher expense ratios, lower volumes, and wider bid-ask spreads. That doesn't make them inherently uninvestable, but they demand a more patient and experienced hand. *Illiquidity isn't a flaw; it's a feature that must be priced in.*

The risk is not just in the countries themselves, but in how the ETFs are structured. Some international ETFs are domiciled in jurisdictions with withholding taxes on dividends or reduced treaty benefits. Others may use synthetic replication to gain access to hard-to-trade markets. Understanding these nuances is essential. For example, an investor might compare two emerging market ETFs with identical index targets but find different outcomes due to tax drag, swap structures, or optimisation algorithms. *Tracking error isn't just an academic metric—it's a real cost to long-term return.*

Yet for all the complexity, the benefits of going global are real and repeatable. Adding non-correlated assets to a portfolio improves its risk-adjusted returns. International equities and bonds often move differently than domestic ones, influenced by different economic cycles, policy regimes, and sector mixes. Over the long term, the ability to draw from a broader opportunity set is a distinct advantage. But it only works if the exposure is deliberate, measured, and maintained through market cycles. Too often, investors chase performance—adding emerging markets after a run-up, only to exit during the inevitable pullback. The result is not diversification but *serial disappointment.*

The question is not whether to invest globally, but how. Should an investor allocate based on GDP weights, market capitalisation, or risk parity? Should emerging markets be treated as a separate asset class or as part of a global blend? There is no singular answer, but there is a requirement for coherence. A portfolio with 90% domestic exposure and a 10% satellite emerging markets ETF may *technically* be diversified, but it is not balanced. Conversely, allocating blindly to international markets without understanding their drivers may introduce more risk than benefit. *Diversification without diligence is a false comfort.*

For some investors, the path forward may involve the use of core-satellite frameworks: using a broad global ETF as a base, supplemented by targeted exposures to countries or regions with distinct advantages. A tilt toward Asia ex-Japan might reflect optimism about demographic growth and technology adoption. A position in Latin American ETFs could hedge against a weakening dollar or rising commodity prices. But these bets should be made consciously, and with awareness that they may underperform for long stretches. *Patience is the price of global participation.*

There is also a philosophical imperative here. Investing globally reflects a belief in openness—not just to different economies, but to different ways of solving problems, growing capital, and adapting to the future. While some investors prefer the familiarity of domestic companies, true diversification requires humility: the willingness to admit that growth, innovation, and resilience are not confined to any single geography. Markets evolve. Frontiers shift. The global investor accepts this—and adjusts accordingly.

The ETF wrapper, in many ways, is the enabler of this worldview. Before the rise of ETFs, accessing international markets meant high fees, limited access, and cumbersome intermediaries. Today, an investor can own a basket of Indonesian banks, Brazilian exporters, or South African telecoms with the click of a button. That's a powerful democratisation of access—but it comes with responsibility. Knowing *what* you own is only the start. Knowing *why* you own it—and how it fits within your overall philosophy—is what separates the allocator from the amateur.

Investing without borders is not about chasing exotic returns. It's about acknowledging that risk is global, opportunity is global, and diversification must be global too. The investor who embraces this will not only build a more resilient portfolio—they will cultivate a broader, more sophisticated understanding of the world itself. That, more than any return metric, is the hallmark of a modern investor.

Chapter 6
The Lazy Portfolio — Radical Simplicity

The most effective investment strategy for the vast majority of people is rarely the one that dazzles with complexity. Its strength lies in endurance. Paradoxically, the more a portfolio strains to be clever, the more vulnerable it becomes. Over-optimisation—like overengineering—introduces fragility. And in the slow, cumulative discipline of investing, fragility can be ruinous.

Enter the "lazy portfolio." The name might sound dismissive at first, but its essence is far from indolence. It is about restraint. It is about deliberately narrowing choices to minimise behavioural error, reduce costs, and amplify consistency. A well-crafted lazy portfolio is no placeholder for the uninformed; it is a sophisticated answer to a profoundly human challenge: the inability to leave well enough alone.

Simplicity's radical power lies not in what it contains, but in its resistance to noise. A two- or three-fund strategy does not lure you into needless trades. It does not demand constant monitoring. It sidesteps the exhausting choreography of sector rotations, market timing, or economic prognostication. Simplicity is protective. Fewer decisions mean fewer opportunities to sabotage your own outcome.

Yet this approach runs counter to the grain of financial culture. Complexity sells. It masks uncertainty. A multi-layered portfolio brimming with exotic funds feels intelligent, even when it is incoherent. Owning just three funds—perhaps a total market equity ETF, a total international ETF, and a bond ETF—feels almost frivolous. Yet evidence, historical and behavioural, repeatedly demonstrates its sufficiency. Often, it outperforms more intricate alternatives once taxes, fees, and timing errors are accounted for.

This chapter does not merely list lazy portfolio templates. It explores *why* they work, and for whom. Popular models—Bogleheads' Three-Fund Portfolio, Ray Dalio's All Weather, the Golden Butterfly—are considered not as recipes but as frameworks. Each encodes a worldview: about volatility, inflation, risk, and resilience. Understanding these underlying assumptions allows you to select, or adapt, a strategy that aligns with both psychology and objectives. The map matters, certainly—but the compass matters more.

One of the lazy portfolio's most profound advantages is scalability. What works with £5,000 scales effortlessly to £5 million. Its structure resists complexity creep. It does not demand quarterly reallocation or a tactical view of the yield curve. It can be automated, delegated, or even ignored for long stretches—quietly compounding in the background. Yet its elegance carries a peculiar vulnerability: it feels *too easy*.

Many investors abandon simplicity not because it fails, but because it ceases to stimulate. The brain craves novelty, and markets provide it. Boredom masquerades as insight. A perfectly sound allocation begins to feel inadequate simply because it lacks drama. This chapter unpacks that psychological trap and explores how to remain intellectually engaged—curious, even—without dismantling the foundation that actually works.

Life-cycle adaptation is another consideration. A lazy portfolio is not one-size-fits-all. While its structure may remain constant, the inputs evolve. A 25-year-old in accumulation requires different weightings than a 60-year-old entering decumulation. Risk tolerance, income needs, and job security shape what is emotionally sustainable. We show how to adjust these portfolios intelligently across life stages, without sacrificing their core advantage: enduring simplicity.

Underlying the lazy portfolio is a quiet philosophy—a refusal to equate effort with outcome, and a resistance to performative complexity. It embodies minimalism, clarity, and intentionality. You need not outrun the market; you need only outlast your impulses. Nothing accomplishes that better than a system that asks very little of you while delivering a great deal in return.

Ultimately, the lazy portfolio is not a compromise. It is a design solution rooted in humility. It acknowledges that markets are unpredictable, behaviour is fallible, and complexity is seductive yet often counterproductive. This chapter invites a shift in perspective:

a "smart" portfolio is not defined by the levers it pulls, but by how little intervention it requires. Less, when intentional, can indeed be more.

Whether early in your career, entering retirement, or simply weary of chasing sophistication for its own sake, this chapter provides the insight—and the discipline—to build a portfolio that is quiet, resilient, and remarkably effective. Not through effort, but through design.

Why Fewer Funds Can Beat More

Complexity in investing often masquerades as sophistication. A portfolio holding twenty or thirty different funds, each covering a nuanced corner of the market, gives the illusion of expert tailoring—of risk deftly allocated, returns finely optimised. But beneath the surface, it is usually a monument to overthinking. Excessive diversification, redundant holdings, costly overlaps, tax inefficiency, and the subtle drag of indecision all conspire to reduce—not enhance—long-term performance. *The truth is disarming: fewer funds, when chosen wisely, frequently outperform more elaborate constructions—not despite their simplicity, but because of it.*

There is a psychological comfort in layers. Investors reach for new funds the way some people rearrange furniture when they feel unproductive—it creates the impression of progress. But adding more slices to a portfolio rarely alters its fundamental exposure. It often results in what is known as "diworsification": a dilution of clarity and conviction in favour of misplaced thoroughness. A portfolio with a total US market ETF and a separate S&P 500 ETF, for instance, doesn't improve diversification—it simply double-counts the same exposure. The same holds for holding multiple international equity funds that largely track overlapping benchmarks. *More is only better when it's meaningfully different.*

The alternative—what many call a "lazy portfolio"—typically consists of two or three carefully selected funds. A global stock market ETF. A bond ETF tailored to your risk tolerance. Perhaps a small allocation to international or emerging markets, if needed.

That's it. Such a structure might sound underwhelming, but it has several embedded advantages that compound over time.

First, simplicity slashes behavioural risk. One of the biggest threats to investor returns is the investor themselves. Reacting emotionally to market volatility, tinkering in response to headlines, or chasing recent performance all result in lower realised returns. A simple portfolio, precisely because it offers fewer levers to pull, discourages tampering. This is not a minor feature—it is a foundational strength. *The fewer decisions a portfolio demands, the fewer opportunities there are for mistakes.*

Second, a minimal portfolio is inherently more tax efficient. With fewer moving parts, there are fewer chances to trigger capital gains unintentionally. Rebalancing is easier to execute with lower tax friction and administrative hassle. Likewise, tracking overall exposure and risk becomes straightforward. This clarity has real-world implications: it enables more consistent behaviour, better planning, and fewer surprises.

There is also the question of fees. While fund-level fees have decreased across the industry, complexity often introduces hidden costs. Owning multiple niche ETFs can mean exposure to higher expense ratios, wider bid-ask spreads, and additional trading costs. A portfolio built on just a few broad-based, low-cost ETFs typically incurs some of the lowest aggregate fees in the investing universe. Over decades, these savings become a meaningful portion of the final outcome. *Cost is not just a line item—it's a compounding force working for or against you.*

Critically, simplicity also reduces decision fatigue. Each additional fund represents a node in the portfolio that must be understood, monitored, and rebalanced. This mental overhead is subtle, but cumulative. It creates drag. Investors report feeling more anxiety, not less, as the number of holdings increases—especially during periods of uncertainty. Portfolio construction then becomes a cognitive burden rather than a tool of empowerment. *The elegance of a minimalist strategy lies in its sustainability.* It's something a person can actually follow—not just when the markets are rising, but when conviction is tested.

Consider the Bogleheads Three-Fund Portfolio: total US equities, total international equities, and total bonds. It is widely criticised by financial pundits for being "too simplistic" or "not tactical enough." Yet time and again, it outperforms more complex arrangements once behavioural errors, turnover, and fees are included in the equation. It's not that the three-fund model is perfect—it's that it removes more sources of error than it introduces. And that, in investing, is a form of excellence.

There are, of course, contexts in which more segmentation may be justified. Institutions with dedicated teams and algorithmic execution models might benefit from more granular slicing—say, splitting out mid-caps from large-caps, or targeting specific geographic tilts. But for most individual investors—even those who are thoughtful, educated, and engaged—adding that level of precision rarely adds value. Instead, it introduces more opportunities to be wrong.

This is not to say that every minimalist portfolio is automatically superior. A portfolio with three expensive, actively managed funds would be worse than a complex one built from disciplined, low-cost tools. But when simplicity is combined with *quality*—that is, low-cost, broadly diversified, transparent ETFs—it becomes a formidable investment engine. It enables something rare in the world of finance: *long-term alignment between strategy and behaviour.*

A common objection is that minimalist portfolios underperform during specific phases of the market. For example, a simple 60/40 stock-bond mix may lag during periods of rapid technological innovation or commodity booms. But that critique misses the point. Portfolios are not designed to win every year. They are designed to *endure*, to compound across regimes, and to reduce the odds of catastrophic failure. In that light, what matters is not whether a simple portfolio outpaces the hot theme of the month—it's whether it delivers its intended risk-adjusted return *with the least need for interference.*

Moreover, there is strong academic backing for the idea that portfolios with a limited number of diversified holdings are harder to beat. The Sharpe ratio—the metric that assesses risk-adjusted returns—doesn't reward you for extra complexity. It penalises volatility and inconsistency. The fewer moving parts, the more stable the trajectory. And as investors, we live and die not by theoretical returns, but by realised ones—those we can actually capture and retain.

This matters even more in retirement. As investors transition from accumulation to decumulation, the last thing they need is an intricate, fragile structure that requires constant oversight. A two- or three-fund model is not only easier to manage, but also easier to communicate to partners, heirs, or advisors. In this way, simplicity is also a form of stewardship.

The ultimate virtue of fewer funds is not that they win every backtest. It's that they make it *more likely you will stick with the plan.* This is what matters most. A sophisticated strategy you cannot follow is worse than a basic one you can. The best portfolio isn't the one with the most complexity—it's the one you actually hold, through thick and thin.

In the end, simplicity scales. It scales across account sizes, market cycles, and emotional states. It is robust under pressure, low-maintenance in practice, and adaptable over time. To choose a two- or three-fund portfolio is not to settle for less. It is to *demand more* from your strategy: more clarity, more alignment, and more durability. Not every solution needs to be complicated. Some need only to be *right.*

Popular Lazy Portfolios: A Comparative Map

A well-built lazy portfolio is a quiet act of rebellion against an industry that thrives on noise. It refuses to chase alpha, micromanage asset classes, or jump in and out of trends. Instead, it commits to structural integrity, to time-tested allocation, and—crucially—to the psychological sustainability required for long-term success. And yet, even within the philosophy of simplicity, not all lazy portfolios are created equal. Some lean into global diversification, others rely on economic regime theory, and a few experiment with gold and unconventional hedges. To understand these models properly, we need to examine not just their composition, but the thinking that underpins them: what they prioritise, who they serve, and how they behave under stress.

Start with the Bogleheads Three-Fund Portfolio. Named for the late John C. Bogle, founder of Vanguard and pioneer of index investing, this portfolio is built around three total market funds: US stocks, international stocks, and bonds. Its appeal is straightforward—it offers comprehensive global exposure, low costs, and minimal maintenance. The equity portion gives access to thousands of companies worldwide, while the bond component dampens volatility and provides income. For many investors, especially those with a long time horizon and moderate risk tolerance, this is a complete solution. *It's not flashy, but it works—because it aligns with the real challenge of investing: staying invested.*

What makes the Bogleheads model resilient isn't precision; it's coverage. By owning total market indices, it avoids the need to pick sectors, geographies, or styles. There's no tilt toward growth or value, no second-guessing over which country or company will lead. This removes the temptation to tinker. Rebalancing once a year is often enough. The model's power lies in its neutrality—its refusal to play favourites—and this makes it unusually hard to sabotage. *If your biggest edge is behavioural discipline, then your portfolio should make discipline easier, not harder.*

Contrast that with the All-Weather Portfolio, developed by Ray Dalio and popularised for retail investors through various interpretations. This model takes a more economic view, allocating assets based on how they are expected to perform across four hypothetical environments: rising growth, falling growth, rising inflation, and falling inflation. Typically, it might include 30% stocks, 40% long-term bonds, 15% intermediate-term bonds, 7.5% gold, and 7.5% commodities. The result is a portfolio that's far more tilted toward stability and downside protection.

The All-Weather approach appeals to a different kind of investor—one who values smoother returns over decades and is wary of concentrated equity risk. During periods of equity volatility, this model has often shown remarkable steadiness. But there are trade-offs. Returns in bull markets can lag. The allocation to long-dated bonds, in particular, becomes a liability during rate hikes or inflationary pressure. Moreover, replicating the All-Weather model with ETFs requires nuance, particularly with commodities and inflation hedges, where costs and tracking quality vary widely. *The model offers philosophical robustness, but only to those willing to understand its inner machinery.*

Then there is the Golden Butterfly Portfolio, a modernised version of the classic Permanent Portfolio originally proposed by Harry Browne. The Golden Butterfly typically consists of 20% total stock market, 20% small-cap value stocks, 20% long-term bonds, 20% short-term bonds, and 20% gold. The underlying thesis is diversification not just by asset class, but by economic function—growth, safety, income, and hard assets. It's a portfolio for the sceptic: someone who distrusts central banks, expects geopolitical shocks, and believes that equity markets are not always rational or rewarding.

This model tends to perform well during stagflationary periods or prolonged volatility. The allocation to gold and short-term bonds creates ballast during drawdowns, while small-cap value adds historical return premium in growth cycles. But it's not a set-and-forget solution. Gold brings tracking challenges and no income. Small-cap value can suffer long periods of underperformance. And the split bond allocation introduces interest rate risk management into the mix. The Golden Butterfly is psychologically stabilising *if* you believe in its premise; otherwise, its conservatism can feel like missed opportunity.

Each of these lazy portfolios works—but only within the context of the investor's psychology, time frame, and convictions. The Bogleheads model is ideal for broad-based optimists who believe in global capitalism and don't want to meddle. The All-Weather suits macro-minded individuals who are concerned about economic cycles and want protection more than participation. The Golden Butterfly fits contrarians, real asset advocates, and those who prioritise capital preservation above all else. *The right lazy portfolio is not the one with the highest theoretical return. It's the one whose logic you can respect even when results deviate from expectations.*

Beyond theory, there are also practical considerations. The Bogleheads model is the easiest to implement using low-cost ETFs with high liquidity. It has minimal tax complexity and scales well across account sizes. The All-Weather and Golden Butterfly models often require more specific instruments—commodities funds, gold ETFs, or duration-targeted bonds—which may have higher costs, lower liquidity, or tracking mismatches. These are not reasons to avoid them, but they are reminders that implementation matters. A great model executed poorly is inferior to a good model implemented consistently.

Another dimension to compare is how each portfolio interacts with rebalancing. The Bogleheads Three-Fund tends to drift with market direction, requiring simple annual rebalancing back to fixed ratios. The All-Weather model, being more finely balanced across macro regimes, can be distorted quickly by strong moves in bonds or equities, requiring more frequent attention. The Golden Butterfly—due to the volatile behaviour of gold and small-cap value—can look unbalanced within a few months. This doesn't necessarily mean higher risk, but it does require a framework: when to rebalance, how strictly, and whether to use thresholds or calendar schedules. *The success of a lazy portfolio depends less on its static structure and more on the integrity of its maintenance.*

Importantly, none of these models are perfect. They all reflect trade-offs. What they share, however, is an intentional relationship between design and behaviour. They aim to create a stable anchor for an investor's decision-making. They simplify the ecosystem of choices. And they all acknowledge—implicitly or explicitly—that the greatest drag on performance is not market returns, but *human inconsistency*. This is their true function: not just allocation, but adherence.

Choosing between these models is not about numerical superiority. Backtests are abundant and contradictory. Historical simulations will always favour certain blends depending on the window selected. But investors don't live in spreadsheets—they live in uncertainty. The real test of a portfolio is whether it can be held in the face of that uncertainty. Lazy portfolios shine not because they guarantee optimal performance, but because they improve *investor outcomes.*

That's a subtler, harder metric to optimise—but a far more meaningful one.

The comparative map of lazy portfolios shows us that there is no universal best. There are only portfolios that serve specific values. The Bogleheads model embodies low-cost, high-trust simplicity. The All-Weather seeks macro neutrality and regime resilience. The Golden Butterfly expresses scepticism of systems and reverence for diversification beyond finance. Each reflects a different answer to the same question: *How can I build wealth without losing my nerve?*

For thoughtful investors, understanding these models is more than academic. It's the start of alignment—between beliefs, behaviour, and structure. Lazy portfolios are not about doing less; they are about doing what matters, and only that. They are humble enough to let markets work, disciplined enough to minimise errors, and robust enough to withstand the long march of time. Whether you choose three funds or five, the essence is the same: *simplicity is not the absence of strategy—it is the outcome of clarity.*

Customising for Your Season of Life

The idea that a portfolio should remain static over a lifetime is a dangerous oversimplification masquerading as discipline. Asset allocation is not just a mathematical exercise—it is a reflection of your psychological capacity, personal goals, earning power, and obligations as they evolve through life. A portfolio that feels comfortable at 30 may feel reckless at 55. Conversely, what seems prudent at 60 might have been suffocatingly conservative at 25. *Investing is not merely about risk tolerance; it's about life alignment.*

Yet conventional investment advice still too often leans on one-size-fits-all heuristics. "100 minus your age equals your stock allocation." Or: "Everyone should own bonds for safety." These are not inherently wrong, but they are intellectually lazy. They fail to engage with the texture of real lives—where income is irregular, children arrive unexpectedly, inheritances complicate planning, careers change trajectory, and health shocks upend priorities. A meaningful approach to lazy portfolio construction must be *adaptive*, not reactive. It must anticipate the investor's changing reality and build with intention.

In early adulthood—roughly ages 20 to 35—time is your greatest asset. The dominant risk isn't market volatility, but *not being in the market at all.* With decades ahead before drawdowns become consequential, an equity-heavy allocation is not just tolerable; it's optimal. A minimalist two-fund or three-fund portfolio that blends total global equities and a small dose of bonds (or none at all) is structurally sound. Costs are low. Decisions are few. Emotional engagement with the market can be developed in a low-stakes environment. But more importantly, these years are for *habituation*—automating contributions, learning how markets behave, and seeing volatility as feature, not bug. *A young investor's greatest advantage is not high returns—it's uninterrupted compounding.*

As you move into your 30s and early 40s, complexity increases. Career paths become clearer or more volatile, family structures are formed, and major expenses—housing, education, caregiving—begin to shape financial decisions. Here, a static portfolio becomes more fragile. Risk tolerance may remain, but *risk capacity*—the ability to absorb loss without jeopardising life goals—begins to shift. Lazy portfolios in this stage benefit from customisation around goal timelines. If a house deposit is needed in five years, a sub-allocation to short-term bonds or cash-like instruments makes sense, even if long-term equity exposure remains high.

This period is also when investors are most prone to *performance envy.* As income increases and financial media becomes louder, the temptation to "optimise" grows. Sector ETFs, thematic plays, and portfolio tinkering often masquerade as sophistication. But the core task here is *segmentation.* A well-structured lazy portfolio may now include a core-satellite model: a passive three-fund base, with modest exposure to high-conviction ideas or hedge positions. The key is containment—experimentation without destabilising the whole.

By the time investors reach their 50s and 60s, the stakes become existential. Retirement stops being abstract. Portfolio drawdowns feel personal. Here, the shift is from accumulation to *preservation.* But again, the answer is not to abandon equities entirely—it's to resize their role in proportion to withdrawal timing, not just age. A 55-year-old planning to work until 70 has a very different portfolio profile than one retiring at 60. Lazy portfolios at this stage often evolve toward income-aware strategies: larger allocations to dividend-paying equities, short-duration bonds, or inflation-protected securities.

The classic 60/40 stock-bond mix may still work—but even this requires nuance. For example, retirees heavily reliant on their portfolios for income should be cautious about duration risk in bonds during rising rate environments. Similarly, overexposure to dividend stocks may reduce diversification. *The discipline of simplicity should not become rigidity.* The best portfolios are still lazy in structure—but conscious in calibration.

Longevity adds a further layer. In an era where retirement may last 30+ years, the portfolio must still grow, not just preserve. Inflation, healthcare costs, and uneven market cycles demand that even retirees hold equities—perhaps 30–50% depending on personal context. Bucket strategies become useful here: separating near-term spending needs from long-term growth pools. But lazy doesn't mean underthought. A retiree's portfolio must still be a living, breathing reflection of evolving needs. Regular check-ins—not constant fiddling—are what sustain it.

Beyond age, *goal-based investing* is an even more precise axis of portfolio design. Saving for a home, funding a child's education, building intergenerational wealth—each goal has its own time horizon, liquidity need, and psychological importance. A high-earning 40-year-old might run three lazy portfolios simultaneously: one aggressive for retirement, one conservative for a child's tuition in 8 years, and one intermediate for semi-retirement or travel. The genius of the lazy portfolio lies in its replicability. It can be cloned, scaled, and targeted—without complexity escalating exponentially.

But even the best designs will falter if the investor does not adapt behaviourally. The temptation to fix what isn't broken grows with age. A 45-year-old with a portfolio that's doubled since their 30s may begin to question whether simplicity is still justified. Shouldn't they be doing something "more advanced"? But often, that urge is not about the portfolio—it's about identity. Success brings expectations. Complexity becomes performative. *But the market does not reward the investor who appears smartest. It rewards the one who makes the fewest costly mistakes.*

The antidote is not austerity—it's intentional design. Building a portfolio that evolves with your life means more than tweaking allocations. It means examining your assumptions. At 25, you may be comfortable with 100% equities—but have you tested that in a real downturn? At 55, you may feel the urge to overcorrect—are you projecting fear, or responding to data? The portfolio should change not just because your age changes, but because your *circumstances and clarity have improved.*

This is why regular reviews matter—not to trigger constant action, but to surface meaningful shifts. Has your time horizon shortened? Has your income volatility changed? Have new dependents emerged? These are the drivers of customisation, not media narratives or market fads. The best investors are not static, but *self-aware.*

And finally, a word on what not to do. Don't use "life stage" as a licence to overhaul the entire structure. Drastic reallocations in response to birthdays or bear markets are often counterproductive. Changes should be evolutionary, not revolutionary. If your portfolio was well-designed to begin with, adjustments should feel like refinements—not rescues.

What this all amounts to is a reframing: a lazy portfolio is not lazy at all. It is quiet precision. Its simplicity belies its depth—because it forces clarity. It invites you to answer the harder questions: not "What's the market doing?" but "What do I need my money to do?" And that answer will shift over time. Your life is not a spreadsheet, and your portfolio should not pretend otherwise. But with conscious adaptation, honest reflection, and a commitment to minimalism with purpose, you can build an investment structure that grows with you—not just in size, but in wisdom.

What to Do When It Feels Too Easy

There's a peculiar discomfort that often follows competence. Once an investor adopts a sound, well-structured portfolio—one that's low-cost, diversified, and grounded in long-term principles—a surprising emotion can creep in: *boredom.* Not the kind born of ignorance, but the kind bred from clarity. No more panicked tinkering, no urgency to beat the market, no roulette wheel of fads to chase. And so, paradoxically, just as investors approach optimal behaviour, they may begin to self-sabotage in search of stimulation. *The portfolio is working—but it no longer feels like they are.*

This phenomenon isn't trivial. It strikes thoughtful, intelligent investors more often than it does reckless ones. Complexity has a psychological allure. The more educated someone is, the more tempted they are to "improve" a plan that is already functioning precisely as it should. There's a certain humility required to maintain a passive three-fund portfolio year after year, ignoring noise and resisting the siren calls of optimisation. Simplicity demands restraint—but more than that, it demands *maturity.*

The problem arises when intellectual boredom masquerades as analytical curiosity. You begin reading more white papers. You start questioning whether factor tilts could enhance your returns. You hear about long volatility strategies or dividend harvesting or trend-following overlays, and wonder whether you're leaving money on the table. The lazy portfolio—once liberating—now feels like an underachievement. But what's actually happening is not a failure of the strategy. It's a failure of narrative engagement. *The story your portfolio tells no longer feels heroic enough.*

To counter this, the solution is not to abandon simplicity, but to *recontextualise it.* Rather than seeking stimulation through portfolio changes, channel your intellectual energy into understanding why your system works. Read deeply about market history. Study the empirical failures of active management. Engage with critiques of passive investing—not to be persuaded, but to refine your conviction. Learn about behavioural finance, not just asset allocation. This shift in focus—from portfolio manipulation to investment philosophy—preserves both intellectual engagement and portfolio integrity.

It also helps to remember that simplicity scales *precisely because* it appears underwhelming. Great systems often look unremarkable in real time. They don't require heroics. They don't make headlines. But they compound. They persist. They avoid the drag of friction and the tax of constant decision-making. The "easy" feeling is actually a signal of system health. And resisting the urge to meddle is itself an act of discipline.

For those who still crave intellectual stimulation, there are legitimate outlets that don't require changing your portfolio. Track your net worth and savings rate with rigour. Build models to explore hypothetical market scenarios. Dive into macroeconomic analysis—not to trade on it, but to deepen your contextual understanding. Develop your skills in tax strategy or estate planning. Each of these can offer intellectual reward without triggering portfolio drift. *You can be fascinated by markets without trying to outsmart them.*

Alternatively, if you genuinely feel under-allocated to creativity, consider allocating a very small portion—1% to 5% of your portfolio—to a sandbox account. This is not for serious capital growth. It's a controlled outlet for experimentation, curiosity, and emotional engagement. You can test thematic ETFs, explore private markets, or tactically trade a sector you understand. The key is containment. This sandbox is a pressure valve, not a blueprint. It exists to protect the *core* of your portfolio from the consequences of boredom.

There's also a psychological reframe worth embracing. When your investment plan feels dull, remember that its purpose is not entertainment. Your investments are not there to thrill you. They are there to *fund your freedom.* That might mean a future without employment dependency, the ability to support family members, the resources to pursue creative projects without financial strain. If you need excitement, go climb a mountain. If you need meaning, go mentor someone. But don't seek it in your ETF allocations.

The most successful investors often appear disinterested in their portfolios—not because they are careless, but because the design is so aligned with their needs that there is little left to question. These individuals have internalised what many overlook: *the purpose of investing is not to feel smart, but to make smart unnecessary.* Once the correct scaffolding is in place, continual effort becomes counterproductive.

This also highlights a more existential tension. In many professions, progress is tied to effort. More time, more input, more advancement. But investing punishes that logic. The more you tinker, the more fees you incur. The more decisions you make, the more chances you have to be wrong. So it creates a kind of dissonance. Hard work elsewhere is rewarded; in investing, *inaction is often the optimal move.* Accepting this can feel anti-instinctual, especially for high achievers. But learning to *separate effort from outcome* is one of the most powerful psychological breakthroughs a disciplined investor can reach.

There's a final layer worth exploring. Many investors use activity to mask anxiety. Doing something—anything—feels better than doing nothing, especially during periods of market volatility. But this is precisely when action is most dangerous. The market falls, and simplicity starts to feel negligent. You want to hedge, to adjust, to protect. But the very design of a lazy portfolio anticipates this. It is built with volatility in mind. Its success lies not in avoiding downturns, but in riding through them undisturbed. *If you've chosen your allocations wisely, boredom during drawdowns is not a sign of negligence—it is a sign of alignment.*

In this context, the real skill is not to add complexity, but to *build confidence in simplicity.* That requires narrative strength: a clear, internalised understanding of why your portfolio is constructed the way it is. It requires intellectual resilience: the capacity to engage with conflicting opinions without being derailed. And it requires behavioural rigour: the ability to observe noise without reacting to it.

Ultimately, if your portfolio ever begins to feel too easy, remind yourself that this is not a flaw—it is the *feature you worked so hard to earn.* Simplicity is not the starting point for beginners. It is the *destination for experts.* Not because they couldn't do more—but because they've learned not to.

Chapter 7
Global Eyes, Local Hands: Investing Internationally

Every investor begins close to home. Early on, trust is local: the domestic economy, familiar companies, the national currency, and the regulatory framework provide a sense of security. Yet, over time, that security can prove illusory. Markets stagnate, industries falter, and currencies lose purchasing power. The investor who never ventures beyond domestic borders discovers that loyalty to home turf is not a guaranteed reward. True diversification does not merely scatter risk; it forces recognition of the risks inherent in remaining insular in an interconnected world.

Global investing is not a luxury reserved for the sophisticated; it is a necessity for the rational. A portfolio that ignores international exposure is not merely incomplete—it is vulnerable to blind spots. Economies rise and fall, sometimes over decades. Japan's lost decades, the eurozone debt crisis, post-Brexit uncertainties in the UK, and the cyclicality of Canada's resource-heavy markets all serve as reminders that geographic concentration is a gamble, not a strategy. In contrast, broad global exposure allows investors to participate in growth wherever it occurs, not just where they reside.

Yet most portfolios remain remarkably domestic. This is rarely ignorance; it is home bias—the subconscious overweighting of domestic assets, justified by comfort, familiarity, or perceived informational advantage. American investors, for example, often hold 70–80% of their equities at home, despite the US representing barely over half of global market capitalisation. British investors cling to the FTSE, Australians favour mining and banking, Japanese portfolios tilt heavily toward domestic equities. It is inertia masquerading as prudence, not patriotism.

International investing is not synonymous with exotic speculation; it is about completing the picture. The global economy generates technological breakthroughs, demographic growth, and sectoral innovation no single country can monopolise. To ignore it is not cautious—it is limiting. ETFs tracking international markets—from MSCI World and FTSE All-World funds to regional or country-specific instruments—offer an accessible, cost-effective means of incorporating this exposure into even the simplest portfolios.

Nonetheless, global investing introduces genuine complexity. Currency risk is immediate and often underestimated. Holding a fund denominated in sterling but invested in eurozone equities means returns are influenced not only by market performance but also by currency fluctuations. Gains may be magnified—or muted. Hedging decisions hinge on time horizon, volatility tolerance, and investment purpose. A retiree drawing income in sterling faces different considerations than a globally mobile entrepreneur.

Political and regulatory risk adds further nuance. Emerging markets can introduce sudden capital controls, governance shifts, or nationalisations unimaginable in developed economies. Even mature markets are not immune: unexpected taxation changes or retroactive policies in France, India, or elsewhere illustrate the point. Such realities are not reasons to avoid foreign markets—they are reasons to engage with awareness. Understanding how ETFs manage country weighting, rebalancing, and liquidity in these contexts is part of prudent diligence.

Perhaps the most dangerous misconception is viewing international exposure as optional rather than foundational. Global diversification is not a supplementary layer for the sophisticated; it is core to a resilient long-term portfolio. The goal is not to outperform neighbours but to endure beyond the cycles of any single economy.

This does not mean abandoning domestic assets. Strategic domestic allocation remains valid, serving tax efficiency, currency alignment, or personal conviction. The key distinction lies in intention: preference should be deliberate, not default.

This chapter begins by examining home bias historically and its consequences—why even strong domestic markets can underperform for decades, and how global ETFs mitigate national underperformance. We then unpack the mechanics of international investing: currency dynamics, geopolitical risks, emerging and frontier markets. Readers will learn to decode ETF labels, evaluate underlying holdings, and choose appropriately among global, regional, or single-country strategies.

We will also confront the perception that international investing is too volatile or complex for everyday investors. With low-cost, all-in-one global ETFs, accessibility is no longer the barrier. What matters is comprehension: knowing what you own, why it matters, and how it complements the broader asset allocation. Simplicity and sophistication coexist; the best international portfolios are straightforward in design but nuanced in exposure.

Psychology too plays a role. Investing abroad feels distant, abstract. National pride offers little incentive in holding Taiwanese semiconductors or Scandinavian banks. Yet, over decades, the question is not where you live—it is where growth will thrive. That may not be your backyard, and even if it is, you need other backyards to ensure resilience.

Transitioning from domestic to global investing fosters a philosophical shift. Investors begin to think not as consumers of national markets, but as citizens of capital. Financial security becomes linked to productivity worldwide—entrepreneurs in Nairobi, engineers in Shenzhen, scientists in Zurich. International investing is not a bet on others; it is recognition that the world's activity is already shaping your future, whether acknowledged or not.

By the end of this chapter, readers will have the tools to navigate global exposure with clarity and intention. You will understand how to select ETFs that combine global opportunity with local practicality, how to manage genuine risks without paralysis, and why international diversification is not optional but foundational.

To construct a portfolio for the world as it is, you must invest beyond the borders you call home. The most consequential boundaries are no longer geographic—they reside in the composition of your portfolio. It is time to cross them.

The Case for Global Exposure

Investors often mistake familiarity for safety. The country you live in—its economy, its companies, its currency—feels more knowable than markets halfway across the world. But comfort is not diversification. Nor is it a defence against systemic decline. A portfolio overly reliant on a single national market, no matter how stable it appears, is not diversified in any meaningful sense—it is concentrated, exposed, and, over time, likely underperforming. *Global exposure isn't an enhancement; it's a correction.*

The notion that domestic markets can be relied upon indefinitely for both growth and protection is contradicted by history, data, and the evolution of global capitalism. Consider the Japanese equity market. At the height of its bubble in 1989, Japan made up roughly 45% of global stock market capitalisation. Investors inside Japan were not simply confident—they believed they were the future. Yet more than three decades later, the Nikkei 225 has still not returned to those heights. An investor who remained fully invested in Japan during that time forfeited opportunity not just in the United States, but in Germany, China, Taiwan, India, and dozens of other markets that surged while Japan stagnated. This is not a cautionary tale about Japan. It's a permanent reminder that *no market is immune to stagnation.*

Nor is Japan an isolated case. UK equities have experienced extended periods of underperformance relative to global indices. Canada, overly weighted in commodities and financials, exhibits high cyclical volatility. Even the United States, dominant as it seems today, has gone through entire decades where it lagged behind international peers. The 2000s—sometimes called the "lost decade" for US equities—saw the S&P 500 deliver negative total returns over ten years, while emerging markets and non-US developed markets surged. Investors who diversified globally during that period not only saw better performance, but smoother risk-adjusted returns. *Geographic diversification is time diversification.*

It is easy, especially during bull markets, to mistake the recent outperformance of US stocks for a structural truth. But performance leadership rotates. From 1985 to 2000, Japan's stock market outpaced the US. From 2003 to 2007, emerging markets vastly outperformed developed markets. From 2010 onward, US tech giants pulled American indices far ahead. But that dominance is not destiny—it is cyclicality. Investors who believe that the past decade is a blueprint for the next are not investing—they're extrapolating. And extrapolation is not a strategy.

Global ETFs exist to break this illusion. Rather than relying on country-specific mutual funds or foreign brokerage accounts, investors today can gain seamless access to hundreds of international equities through a single, low-cost product. An MSCI World ETF offers exposure to over 1,500 large- and mid-cap companies across 23 developed markets. A FTSE All-World tracker includes emerging markets alongside developed economies, capturing nearly 95% of the global investable universe. These are not exotic products. They are foundational tools for any investor who recognises that the world is bigger than their postcode.

Still, scepticism persists. One argument holds that investing globally increases volatility, citing currency fluctuations, political instability, or uneven corporate governance. It's a fair concern, but it misunderstands *net portfolio effect.* While individual foreign markets may be volatile, the aggregate effect of owning many markets tends to reduce overall volatility—because different economies do not move in lockstep. Currency movements can be volatile, yes. But for long-term investors, the unhedged exposure can also act as a natural diversifier, smoothing returns when domestic markets falter. A weak pound, for example, boosts the value of international holdings denominated in dollars or euros, acting as a partial hedge against local economic weakness.

Moreover, assuming that domestic markets are inherently more stable is a false comfort. Political risk is not a developing-world phenomenon. The UK's rapid leadership changes, Brexit's economic fallout, the US debt ceiling debates, or eurozone fragmentation—these are all advanced-economy risks. When you invest globally, you don't remove risk—you spread it. And *spread risk is absorbed risk.*

The second layer of misunderstanding around global exposure is the belief that it's "nice to have" rather than necessary. Many investors build their portfolios around a domestic core, then bolt on international funds at the margins—as if they were seasoning, not substance. This fails to account for the role that foreign equities play in *long-term resilience.* They provide access to different demographic trends, commodity cycles, regulatory environments, innovation hubs, and even consumption cultures. Consider South Korea's dominance in semiconductors, Switzerland's global pharmaceutical giants, India's IT outsourcing sector, or Brazil's agribusiness strength. These are engines of global growth that will operate regardless of your local stock exchange.

Indeed, as economic power shifts East and South in the 21st century, the most dynamic returns may come from markets that were once dismissed as peripheral. The growth of middle classes in Asia, the rise of tech ecosystems in Africa, and the development of infrastructure in Latin America are not abstractions—they are capital flows, earnings, and dividend streams available to the globally positioned investor. ETFs tracking emerging markets, frontier markets, or regional indices offer scalable and transparent vehicles to tap into this growth—without the idiosyncratic risks of individual stock picking in foreign jurisdictions.

Yet even within global exposure, precision matters. Not all global ETFs are constructed equally. Some overrepresent developed economies, especially the United States, which can reintroduce the very home bias one aims to avoid. Others tilt toward growth stocks, inadvertently replicating the sectoral risks of domestic tech-heavy indices. Thoughtful investors must evaluate the underlying constituents of each fund, the weighting methodology, the currency denomination, and the degree of overlap with existing holdings. *Diversification is not about quantity—it's about correlation.*

To be globally diversified is not simply to *own everything.* It is to own wisely—across geographies, sectors, currencies, and regulatory regimes—with an understanding of how those exposures interact. A well-constructed global allocation enhances risk-adjusted returns not by chasing performance, but by accepting that no one market holds a monopoly on the future.

More subtly, global investing challenges a kind of financial myopia. It compels investors to think beyond the local news cycle, beyond national elections, and beyond familiar companies. It fosters a discipline rooted in humility—an acknowledgment that talent, productivity, and innovation are not confined to borders. That your financial future may depend as much on demographic shifts in Indonesia or interest rate changes in Germany as it does on anything happening in your home country.

Perhaps most importantly, global exposure acts as a counterweight to emotional investing. When your portfolio is diversified across continents, it becomes harder to react impulsively to local panic. A recession in your own country might lead to market drawdowns, job insecurity, or political instability—but if your portfolio holds global assets, the financial impact is buffered. That psychological distance—*between what you feel and what you own*—can be the difference between staying the course and selling at the bottom.

There will always be periods when domestic markets outperform. And there will be temptations to simplify portfolios down to the most recent winner. But investing is not about what worked last quarter. It's about what will endure for the next 20 years. The case for global exposure is not an argument about tactics—it's a statement about *structure*. It's not just another asset class. It is the scaffolding that keeps the whole portfolio upright when one part of the world falters.

To diversify globally is to acknowledge that the world does not revolve around your country's stock exchange. It is to admit that you cannot know in advance where growth will come from, but you can position yourself to receive it—wherever it emerges. It is the ultimate act of humility—and the smartest expression of confidence.

Understanding Currency and Political Risk

International investing offers the promise of enhanced diversification, access to fast-growing economies, and exposure to different business cycles. Yet alongside these benefits comes a spectrum of risks that are often underappreciated, particularly by investors accustomed to the stability of developed domestic markets. Among the most consequential of these are *currency* and *political* risks—two forces that, while distinct in nature, are deeply interconnected and capable of undermining investment performance even when the underlying asset fundamentals remain sound. A portfolio built for global exposure cannot afford to treat these as footnotes. They are not peripheral risks; they are structural variables with systemic implications.

To begin with currency risk, the distinction between *local returns* and *investor returns* is not merely semantic. It is financial reality. When an investor in the UK buys an ETF denominated in US dollars or emerging market currencies, their ultimate return is a combination of the underlying asset performance and the exchange rate movement between sterling and the local currency. A 10% rise in a Brazilian equity fund can evaporate entirely if the Brazilian real depreciates 10% against the pound over the same period. Currency movements can amplify or nullify returns with no relation to the operational results of the companies held. For investors who fail to account for this, surprises are not exceptions—they are baked in.

This does not mean that all currency risk should be hedged. It means it should be *understood and intentional.* Hedging eliminates currency exposure by using financial instruments to neutralise exchange rate effects. But hedging comes at a cost: both explicit, in the form of fees and slippage, and implicit, in the form of reduced diversification benefits. An unhedged global portfolio, though more volatile in the short term, can provide a natural shock absorber in times of domestic weakness—when the home currency falls, the value of foreign holdings rises. Conversely, a hedged portfolio smooths volatility but may underperform over longer time frames, particularly when inflation differentials or interest rate spreads are at play. *The right choice depends on context—specifically the investor's base currency, time horizon, and need for stability versus upside.*

It's important to distinguish between currency volatility and currency *directionality*. While volatility adds noise to short-term performance, directional shifts can erode capital over years. A British investor in 2015 who allocated heavily to US-based assets benefitted significantly from the weakening of the pound post-Brexit. That was not foresight; it was asymmetric exposure that worked in their favour. But the same mechanism works in reverse. An American investing heavily in Japanese equities from 2012 to 2015 would have watched strong corporate performance in Japan entirely offset by a plummeting yen. The implication is not to avoid currency exposure, but to model its potential impact under multiple macroeconomic regimes. *Global investing is not just about what you own—it's about how it translates.*

Currency risk is conceptually easier to grasp than political risk, but the latter can be far more destabilising. Political risk encompasses a wide range of phenomena: regulatory changes, expropriation of assets, capital controls, election uncertainty, shifts in economic policy, and social unrest. These are not academic abstractions. Argentina has repeatedly imposed capital controls that prevented foreign investors from repatriating profits. Russia's invasion of Ukraine in 2022 rendered many of its financial markets uninvestable overnight. China has issued sweeping regulatory interventions in technology, education, and property, wiping out hundreds of billions in market capitalisation. These are not risks you can diversify around *within* a country. They are systemic ruptures—breaks in the contract between capital and the state.

Some political risks are priced into the market—reflected in bond yields, equity valuations, or risk premiums. But many are not. Sudden political upheavals tend to have asymmetric consequences. The downside can be catastrophic; the upside often limited. For example, the potential gains from deregulation or pro-market reforms are rarely as dramatic as the losses that follow from authoritarian crackdowns or arbitrary policy reversals. *Political tail risks are skewed.*

ETFs provide some insulation by spreading exposure across many companies and sectors, but they cannot eliminate country-specific risk. An ETF tracking Turkey or Venezuela will still bear the full impact of any political shock that hits the national economy or investor confidence. And while diversified regional or global ETFs can mitigate the impact of any one country, they may still carry concentrated exposure to politically sensitive jurisdictions—especially if those countries have high weightings due to market capitalisation. Investors need to *look through the label* to the underlying holdings and ask: "What kind of sovereignty risk am I underwriting here?"

One practical approach to navigating political risk is the use of *risk-weighted allocation*, rather than capital-weighted. In other words, instead of allocating purely based on market size, allocate based on volatility, transparency, governance standards, and rule-of-law indices. A capital-weighted global index will be heavy on China due to its sheer market cap. A risk-aware investor might decide that China's opacity and unpredictability warrant a lower weight. Tools like the World Bank's Worldwide Governance Indicators, Transparency International's Corruption Perceptions Index, and Freedom House's democracy ratings can serve as important inputs. These are not foolproof, but they're more informative than backward-looking price charts.

Currency and political risk frequently interact in complex ways. A populist government may devalue its currency to spur exports. A central bank may respond to political interference by hiking interest rates to defend the currency, hurting domestic credit markets. Or geopolitical tensions may trigger capital flight, leading to both political instability and currency collapse. These feedback loops are especially dangerous in emerging markets, where institutions are weaker and investor confidence more fragile. It is not enough to assess these risks in silos—they must be integrated into a coherent view of *macro fragility*.

Investors must also understand the role of *liquidity risk* in amplifying the effects of currency and political instability. During a crisis, markets do not simply decline—they often seize up. Bid-ask spreads widen, foreign capital flees, and domestic investors are paralysed by uncertainty. In these conditions, even ETFs can suffer significant tracking error or price dislocation. In 2018, during Turkey's currency crisis, ETF prices diverged sharply from net asset values, leaving investors exposed not just to market losses, but to execution risk. *Liquidity dries up precisely when you need it most.*

The goal of this section is not to scare investors away from international markets. It is to inoculate them against naïveté. The sophistication of global ETFs does not absolve the investor from responsibility. Due diligence does not end with reading a fund's factsheet. It begins with understanding how the fund's performance is tied to forces beyond spreadsheets: elections, treaties, trade wars, revolutions, monetary policy, sanctions, and nationalism. Currency and political risk are not exotic—they are embedded in the fabric of cross-border investing.

A prudent investor does not avoid risk. They map it. They respect it. They *price* it. And above all, they ensure that it fits the purpose of the portfolio—not just in theory, but in practice. That means knowing whether the risk aligns with the investor's timeline, goals, and tolerance for volatility. A young investor building long-term wealth may accept more exposure to emerging market volatility and currency fluctuations. A retiree seeking income and capital preservation may choose a more hedged, conservative global allocation. There is no universal prescription—only informed positioning.

Currency and political risks are reminders that global investing is not merely a geographic decision; it is a strategic stance on how capital behaves across systems. They require not just analysis, but *perspective.* The investor who appreciates these forces is not necessarily the one who avoids trouble—but they are far more likely to *endure it.*

Home Bias and Its Discontents

Most investors pride themselves on making rational decisions. They study fundamentals, diversify across sectors, and favour low-cost vehicles like ETFs. Yet even the most disciplined portfolios often harbour a hidden distortion: an outsized allocation to the investor's own domestic market. This phenomenon, known as *home bias*, is not merely common—it is ubiquitous. American investors typically allocate upwards of 70% of their equity exposure to U.S. companies, despite the U.S. representing only around 40% of the global stock market by capitalisation. British investors show similar tendencies, with disproportionate exposure to UK equities. Japanese, Canadian, Australian—the pattern repeats. Investors in nearly every developed market prefer the familiar over the global. The consequences are subtle but profound.

At first glance, home bias seems understandable. Investing in domestic companies offers a perceived informational advantage.

One recognises the brands, reads the local financial press, and follows the economy through lived experience. Currency risk is minimised, and taxation is often simpler. There's also a patriotic element at play—a subconscious preference for supporting the local economy. Yet *familiarity is not the same as insight*, and comfort is not a substitute for return. Home bias seduces through the illusion of control, but in doing so, it often sabotages diversification.

One of the foundational principles of modern portfolio theory is that diversification reduces unsystematic risk. But overconcentration in a single country—particularly one's own—leaves a portfolio dangerously exposed to local shocks. Consider the case of Japan in the 1990s. After peaking in 1989, the Nikkei 225 suffered a slow-motion collapse that lasted more than a decade. Japanese investors who stayed exclusively domestic endured stagnation, while those with global exposure had access to the growth of the U.S., Europe, and emerging markets. A similar story unfolded in the UK during the 1970s: rampant inflation, industrial decline, and political instability made local equities a volatile and unreliable store of value. Investors who confined themselves to home markets absorbed full exposure to these macroeconomic events. They weren't just underperforming—they were unhedged.

It's worth asking why investors persist in over-allocating to domestic assets despite the theoretical and empirical case for global diversification. Part of the answer lies in behavioural psychology. Humans exhibit *availability bias*—the tendency to overestimate the probability of events that are most mentally accessible. Domestic stocks dominate local news. Local economic narratives shape perceptions. The result is a myopic view of the investment universe. There is also *status quo bias*—a preference for the familiar state of affairs, even when alternatives offer superior risk-adjusted returns. Inertia becomes the enemy of optimisation.

Regulatory and institutional structures can reinforce home bias. Employer-sponsored pension plans may offer limited international options. Tax incentives often favour domestic funds. Even the design of default investment products, such as target-date retirement funds, frequently underweight international equities. And media coverage, often national in focus, gives disproportionate attention to domestic market events, subtly encouraging investors to equate relevance with proximity. *The design of the system normalises the distortion.*

Home bias is especially problematic in smaller economies with narrow equity markets. A British investor, for example, who allocates heavily to the FTSE 100 is concentrating their exposure in a handful of multinational firms, many of which derive the bulk of their earnings from overseas anyway. This creates a paradox: the investor believes they are betting on the UK, but in reality, they are exposed to global revenue streams through a local lens. Meanwhile, they miss the diversification benefits of owning companies listed elsewhere—firms with different corporate cultures, growth dynamics, and regulatory environments. The same is true for Canadian investors over-relying on financials and natural resources, or Australians overweight in mining and real estate. *Sector concentration and home bias are often two sides of the same coin.*

There are also *currency implications* to consider. A portfolio denominated entirely in local currency may appear less volatile on the surface, but it carries hidden risks—particularly in countries with weaker currencies or more volatile exchange rates. Investors who live and spend in one currency but invest entirely in that same currency are assuming that their economy and currency will always remain stable. This assumption holds—until it doesn't. The UK pound has seen substantial depreciation against the dollar and euro over the past decade. Emerging market currencies are even more prone to sudden devaluation. Diversifying across geographies can also function as a hedge against local currency weakness, offering protection when domestic purchasing power erodes. *Currency is not just a medium of transaction; it is a store of confidence.*

To be clear, a degree of home bias may be justified. Retirees spending in local currency may reasonably wish to avoid excessive foreign exchange volatility. Investors with deep expertise in domestic sectors may find legitimate edge in their local market. And taxation, particularly capital gains treatment and dividend withholding rules, can tilt the balance toward local holdings in specific jurisdictions. But these are tactical considerations, not strategic justifications for structural overexposure. The difference matters.

The irony is that the very ETFs that make global diversification so accessible are often underutilised in retail portfolios. Broad-based international ETFs—such as MSCI World ex-U.S., FTSE Developed ex-U.K., or MSCI Emerging Markets—allow investors to access hundreds or even thousands of companies with a single holding. Costs are low, liquidity is high, and execution is simple. And yet these tools remain sidelined in many portfolios because they are perceived as ancillary rather than essential. *Global exposure should not be a satellite allocation—it should be part of the core.*

Performance data supports this assertion. Over the long term, global portfolios have delivered superior risk-adjusted returns compared to those constrained by national borders. They are less sensitive to single-country recessions, political instability, or regulatory upheaval. They benefit from growth in multiple economies, from demographic booms to technological innovation. And they evolve with the global economy, which is increasingly interconnected. *A globally diversified portfolio reflects not only financial prudence but an understanding of where innovation, productivity, and demand are emerging.*

What's often missed in this conversation is that global diversification is not a bet *against* your home market. It is not an expression of pessimism. It is a recognition of structural realism. No economy, however developed, is immune from stagnation, policy error, or demographic decline. Japan has shown that technological sophistication does not guarantee equity returns. The U.S. may dominate global indices today, but it did not during the 1970s, and it may not tomorrow. By diversifying internationally, the investor is not fleeing from home—they are *stepping outside its gravitational pull.*

Addressing home bias requires both technical and psychological shifts. Technically, it means recalibrating asset allocations to better reflect the global market opportunity set. Psychologically, it means confronting the discomfort of the unfamiliar. It means accepting that owning a Korean semiconductor company or a Danish pharmaceutical firm may be just as rational—and often more productive—than doubling down on local banks or utilities. It means trusting the data, not just the headlines.

Ultimately, home bias is not just a portfolio inefficiency; it's a mirror. It reflects our cognitive defaults, our comfort with the known, our illusion of control. The disciplined investor recognises that diversification is not just a statistical concept—it is a mindset. A global mindset. One that sees beyond flags and borders, and focuses on fundamentals, risk, and resilience. Breaking free of home bias is not simply about reallocating capital. It's about *reframing perspective.* And in doing so, building a portfolio that is not only better diversified, but better prepared for whatever tomorrow brings.

ETFs That Span Borders

The modern investor is no longer confined to their local exchange. With a few keystrokes, capital can traverse continents, sectors, and currencies. Exchange-traded funds that span borders have turned what was once an elite advantage—access to global diversification—into a democratised tool. Yet while the vehicle is accessible, its optimal use is far less intuitive. Not all global ETFs are built the same. And not all complement a core portfolio with equal elegance. The key lies in discernment: understanding what each type of fund captures, what it excludes, and what role it ought to play.

Global ETFs fall broadly into two categories: those that *aggregate* international exposure, and those that *target* it with precision. Aggregators include broad indices such as the MSCI World, FTSE All-World, or MSCI ACWI (All Country World Index). These vehicles pool equities from dozens of countries into a single fund, often weighting constituents by market capitalisation. They offer near-total equity exposure in one instrument—developed markets, emerging economies, and, depending on the index, frontier markets too. Their appeal is simplicity. Their risk is generalisation.

Consider the MSCI World Index, frequently misunderstood by novice investors as a comprehensive global benchmark. In fact, it covers only developed markets—omitting entire regions like Latin America, Eastern Europe, and large swaths of Asia. An investor relying solely on an MSCI World ETF gains substantial exposure to the United States (typically over 60%), followed by Japan, the UK, and other developed European economies. It's diversified, but not complete. The MSCI ACWI corrects for this omission by including emerging markets, yet still retains a market-cap weighting that privileges the largest companies and economies. *The result is a global portfolio that may not be as balanced as it appears.*

Market-cap weighting, for all its benefits in efficiency and scalability, tends to concentrate exposure in dominant markets. In today's context, that means U.S. tech firms occupy a disproportionate share of global ETFs. Apple, Microsoft, and NVIDIA appear not just in domestic indices but also in global benchmarks. The overlap can lead to hidden redundancy—investors who own both a U.S. index fund and a "global" ETF may be doubling up without realising it. The lesson here is not to avoid global ETFs, but to *interrogate what they hold, and how that aligns with your broader asset allocation.*

This raises a core question: what is the role of a global ETF in a well-constructed portfolio? For some investors, it serves as the portfolio itself—one fund to capture the global equity premium, rebalance automatically, and eliminate the temptation to tinker. For others, global ETFs act as ballast: a stabilising layer beneath more active or thematic allocations. In both cases, clarity of intention is critical. Using a global ETF as a core holding demands scrutiny of its construction: Does it include emerging markets? How heavily weighted is it toward the U.S.? What sectors dominate? What is its currency exposure, and how does that interact with your spending currency?

Country-specific and region-specific ETFs, by contrast, are instruments of *deliberate tilt.* They allow investors to express a view—about demographics, valuation, policy, or momentum—in a targeted way. A fund tracking Indian equities, for example, offers access to a high-growth, consumption-led economy with favourable demographics. A Japan ETF may appeal to those betting on corporate governance reform and monetary accommodation. European funds can provide dividend yield and value exposure in a historically cyclical market. But these funds are not substitutes for diversification; they are complements. Their role is not to mirror the global economy but to *accentuate a conviction within it.*

The use of these regional tools comes with added responsibilities. Investors must evaluate not just the macro case, but the ETF's implementation: how it handles local market idiosyncrasies, corporate governance, index methodology, and liquidity. Consider the difference between a cap-weighted China ETF and one that tracks the CSI 300 or MSCI China A Inclusion Index. The former may be dominated by state-owned enterprises listed in Hong Kong; the latter may lean into domestically listed firms with greater retail investor influence. These are not academic distinctions. They shape exposure in material ways. *Precision at the selection level avoids disappointment at the performance level.*

Currency risk is another axis along which global ETFs diverge. Some funds are currency-hedged—neutralising the impact of foreign exchange fluctuations on returns—while others are not. The choice between them is neither obvious nor universal. Hedged funds may reduce volatility, especially in developed market exposure, but can also increase costs and reduce diversification. Unhedged funds expose investors to foreign currency gains or losses, which can work as a tailwind or a drag depending on global macro conditions. Investors who spend in sterling but invest heavily in dollar- or euro-denominated assets need to weigh these risks carefully. *Currency exposure is not just a side effect—it is a portfolio variable in its own right.*

In practice, blending different types of global ETFs can yield the best results. A portfolio anchored by an ACWI fund might be complemented by a small-cap international ETF to access less correlated returns. A developed markets ETF can be balanced with an emerging markets fund, allowing for granular rebalancing and more responsive allocation. This modular approach increases investor agency, but also demands greater intentionality. It resists the seduction of set-it-and-forget-it simplicity while avoiding the chaos of over-fragmentation. *Complexity should always serve clarity—not the other way around.*

It is also essential to view global ETFs not as passive bystanders but as evolving instruments. Index providers periodically rebalance constituents, reclassify countries, or change methodologies. MSCI's decision to gradually increase China A-share weighting is a case in point. FTSE's shifting treatment of Korea as either a developed or emerging market affects fund flows and index structure. Investors must remain aware of such changes—not because they demand immediate action, but because they alter the substance of what a fund represents. *The label may remain the same while the underlying exposure shifts beneath it.*

Another layer of discernment involves cost. While global ETFs are generally low-fee compared to active global mutual funds, costs can vary significantly. Broad ETFs from providers like Vanguard or iShares may charge under 0.10% annually, while specialised international funds may cost 0.30% or more. That difference may seem trivial, but over decades, it compounds. And more importantly, *higher fees must be justified by distinctly different exposure, not merely a fancier name or smaller market niche.* Expense ratios should be viewed in tandem with tracking error, bid-ask spreads, and the fund's underlying liquidity.

For investors seeking sustainability or governance alignment, global ESG ETFs offer a parallel track. These funds apply environmental, social, and governance screens to the global opportunity set. But again, methodology matters. Some ESG ETFs merely exclude tobacco and weapons; others tilt heavily toward tech and away from energy. The result can be an ETF that looks very different from the global index it claims to shadow. Investors must ask not just whether an ETF is ESG, but *how* it is ESG—and what that means for their exposure. *Values-based investing requires values-based due diligence.*

Ultimately, ETFs that span borders offer more than access. They offer *perspective.* By holding companies from São Paulo to Seoul, from Zurich to Johannesburg, the investor aligns their portfolio with the arc of global growth. They sidestep the trap of geographic insularity and engage with a broader economic narrative—one that is increasingly decentralised, multipolar, and dynamic. But such engagement requires more than ownership. It requires understanding. *A global ETF is not just a passport—it is a commitment to the complexity of the world.*

To select wisely, investors must resist the lure of labels and dig into structure, weighting, methodology, and purpose. They must decide whether a fund will serve as anchor or accent, core or satellite. And they must do so not once, but continually—as the markets evolve, as global dynamics shift, and as their own objectives mature. This is not analysis for its own sake. It is stewardship. And it is the difference between owning the world—and actually understanding it.

Chapter 8
How to Actually Buy an ETF

The theory of investing can be exhilarating; the practice, often paralysing. After weeks or months of reading about asset allocation, fund construction, and portfolio philosophy, many first-time investors freeze at a deceptively simple question: how do I actually do this? Not conceptually, but concretely. Which platform? Which ticker? What happens when I click "buy"? For all the sophistication of financial literature, executing a trade remains the moment when theory confronts reality. It is no longer a spreadsheet exercise—it is a decision, loaded with responsibility, uncertainty, and a subtle but undeniable emotional weight. This chapter exists to guide that leap—from understanding to doing.

At first glance, buying an ETF seems trivial. Yet the simplicity is misleading. The initial trade is a psychological threshold: a commitment to priorities, to risk, and to action despite incomplete knowledge. Monetary stakes may be modest—£100 or £1,000 won't topple your finances—but the symbolic significance is profound. This is the point where intellectual understanding meets exposure, and many investors postpone it indefinitely. Not because they lack information, but because they seek reassurance. This chapter does not diminish that anxiety; it equips it.

The first consideration is the platform itself. Today's landscape is vast: sleek, app-based interfaces sit alongside institutional-grade portals. The choice is consequential. It shapes fees, yes, but more subtly, it shapes behaviour. One-click trades, push notifications, gamified dashboards—these nudges can quietly erode the discipline that long-term investing demands. Conversely, a functional, even uninspiring interface can act as a behavioural moat, protecting against noise. Choosing a platform is not just a technical decision; it is a declaration of the kind of investor you wish to become.

Then comes the act of buying, which is often treated as trivial in textbooks. But beneath the surface—ticker symbol, order type, quantity, execution method—lie layers of intention. Market or limit order? Lump sum or phased purchase? Currency denomination and forex implications? Fractional shares, if available—how does that alter approach? These details are not minutiae; they are architecture. A resilient portfolio begins with understanding the mechanics of trades.

Beyond the first trade lies sustainability. One of the most underappreciated forces in long-term wealth building is automation. Not in a tech sense alone, but as a human strategy: removing decision points, smoothing behaviour, and lowering cognitive strain. Dollar-cost averaging (DCA) exemplifies this principle. It is unglamorous and may underperform in a bull market, yet it shields investors from the most dangerous variable in the system: themselves. This chapter offers a realistic DCA schedule—not theoretical, but practicable—and examines when lump-sum investing may make sense, such as with bonuses, inheritances, or windfalls.

Equally important is the question of selling, often neglected or treated as reactive. Selling is not merely the converse of buying—it is its ethical twin. If you purchase with intention, you should sell with intention. The chapter presents a framework for principled exits: life changes, revised horizons, portfolio rebalancing, or structural issues in the fund. It also identifies the traps—boredom, fear, overconfidence, and the illusion of productivity. Investors are not rewarded for trading; they are rewarded for waiting well. And waiting, it turns out, is a skill, not a default.

Platforms offer tools and temptations alike. Real-time charts, leaderboards, and endless ETF suggestions appear helpful, yet are behavioural hazards. Daily portfolio checks subtly encourage reaction over reflection. Establishing an environment that reduces such friction—disabling notifications, removing the app from your phone, reviewing holdings quarterly rather than hourly—is not deprivation; it is disciplined design. Architecture often matters more than willpower.

Throughout, a few themes recur: simplicity over complexity, clarity over cleverness, commitment over perfection. The goal is not the perfect trade, but the first of many. ETF investing is not a singular gesture but a sequence of quiet, deliberate choices that compound over months and years. If this chapter spurs your first purchase, automates contributions, or guides a principled exit, it may prove the most consequential in practice. Not for technical sophistication, but for bridging the hardest gap in finance: the one between knowing and doing.

Ultimately, the objective is not mere execution, but the cultivation of a philosophy of execution—methodical, reflective, and resilient. Expertise is not a prerequisite for buying an ETF well; understanding your commitment, establishing a durable rhythm, and maintaining conviction through boredom, panic, and market noise are. You are not a guest in the markets; you are a participant. The interface may be digital, but the process is deeply human. This chapter is about making it work for you.

Brokers, Apps, and Platforms—What Matters Most

The decision of where to invest is not merely administrative—it is architectural. The platform you choose to access ETFs will shape not only the cost and convenience of your trades but the entire psychology of your investing experience. Investors tend to obsess over portfolio construction, fund selection, and macroeconomic trends. Yet few give equal attention to the interface through which all these ideas are enacted. This is a mistake. In behavioural finance, the environment is not neutral. It nudges, it amplifies, it constrains. Whether you are a first-time buyer or a seasoned allocator, the choice of broker or platform deserves scrutiny not just for what it enables, but for what it prevents.

Most platforms fall into one of three categories: legacy brokers, modern apps, and hybrid platforms. Each has a distinct character, shaped by their founding era, core demographic, and business incentives. Legacy brokers—think Hargreaves Lansdown in the UK or Fidelity in the US—offer depth, trust, and a breadth of services. They appeal to investors who value institutional heft and customer support over minimalism. Their interfaces are often less intuitive, but their custody processes and compliance frameworks are robust. At the opposite end, app-based brokers such as Freetrade, Trading 212, or Robinhood offer speed, ease, and gamified aesthetics. They cater to digital natives who want investing to feel like any other mobile interaction. Somewhere in between lie hybrid platforms such as Vanguard's Investor Platform or AJ Bell, which try to blend credibility with user experience. No one model is inherently superior. But they serve different philosophies. *Your choice should align with your intent, not your impulses.*

The first dimension to examine is cost—but not in the simplistic sense of "cheapest is best." Fees must be understood in context. Platforms typically charge in three ways: account fees (flat or percentage-based), trading commissions (per trade), and fund-specific costs (which are embedded in the ETF). Some low-cost platforms seem attractive upfront but offer a limited ETF universe, or lack tax-efficient wrappers like ISAs and SIPPs. Others may offer extensive features but penalise inactivity or impose steep fees on international trades. The key is to match the platform's pricing model to your investing behaviour. If you're a buy-and-hold investor making quarterly contributions, a flat-fee structure may be optimal. If you're dollar-cost averaging with small sums, commission-free trading becomes essential. The goal is not merely to minimise fees, but to *optimise them against your habits.*

User interface matters more than most people admit. Not because beauty is a virtue in itself, but because friction changes behaviour. A cluttered, data-heavy dashboard can overwhelm a new investor. A minimalist app can obscure vital information. Some platforms offer real-time charting, news feeds, and sentiment indicators—features that seem helpful but often encourage reactive behaviour. Others default to a watchlist or portfolio view, subtly reinforcing a short-term mindset. Good design in an investing context is not about aesthetic delight. It is about *behavioural alignment.* Does the interface nudge you to act often, or think deeply? Does it reward restraint, or mimic social media's dopamine loops? If your platform makes you want to check prices daily, consider the cost—not in pounds, but in peace.

Security is the silent foundation of any investment platform. Most retail investors take it for granted, assuming their money is safe as long as the company is regulated. But regulation is only the first layer. Beneath it are questions of custody, compensation schemes, and operational robustness. Does the platform hold client assets separately from its own? Is it covered by the Financial Services Compensation Scheme (FSCS)? What happens if the platform goes out of business? These are not paranoid questions—they are practical ones. The global financial crisis, the Wirecard scandal, and the collapse of crypto exchanges like FTX remind us that platform risk is real. A trustworthy platform doesn't just manage your investments. It stewards your trust. *That's worth paying for.*

Tax-efficiency is another critical, and often overlooked, feature. In the UK, platforms vary significantly in their support for ISAs, SIPPs, and general investment accounts. Some offer automated tax reporting, others leave it to you. For higher-rate taxpayers, this can be the difference between long-term compounding and a constant tax drag. If you plan to invest through a pension or ISA, your platform must support it without excessive fees or complexity. If you're investing through a general account, look for tools that help you track capital gains and dividend income. Good platforms make tax compliance easy. Great platforms make it invisible.

Range and access are more nuanced than they appear. Some platforms offer a curated list of ETFs, others open the entire universe. Curation can be helpful for novices—it reduces choice overload. But it can also be limiting for investors who wish to access specific regions, sectors, or factor exposures. Look carefully at the ETF availability, especially if you plan to use lesser-known funds like ESG-screened variants, currency-hedged versions, or synthetic replication structures. International investors face another layer of complexity: not all platforms offer access to the same listings. An ETF available on the London Stock Exchange might not be available on a European or Asian platform. Know your geography—and your tax jurisdiction. *Access is not universal, and ignorance is expensive.*

Customer service is rarely prioritised until it is urgently needed. But when trades fail, transfers freeze, or accounts are locked, the quality of human support becomes critical. Some app-based brokers have no call centres—only email queues or chatbots. Others offer dedicated support lines but restrict them to business hours. The question is not just whether you can get help, but whether you can get *useful* help—promptly, clearly, and from someone who understands ETFs. For investors with significant sums or complex situations, this may be a decisive factor. Convenience in good times is easy. Competence in difficult times is rare.

Long-term reliability is more than financial solvency. It is about platform longevity, roadmap clarity, and business incentives. Some brokers exist to serve investors. Others exist to monetise them—through order flow, cross-selling, or speculative "features." Platforms backed by banks or asset managers may have more conservative roadmaps but greater stability. Venture-backed apps may innovate rapidly, but pivot just as fast. Look not only at today's offering, but at tomorrow's alignment. What is the platform optimising for—your growth, or their engagement metrics? If the answer is not obvious, the costs may be hidden.

Behavioural design deserves its own mention. Some platforms are intentionally boring. They discourage excessive trading, suppress price alerts, and emphasise long-term goals. Others are explicitly built to increase usage—through nudges, badges, or FOMO-inducing metrics. The latter may not charge you in fees, but they extract value in attention. A good platform helps you become the investor you aspire to be. A bad one trains you to chase noise. Choose accordingly. *Your future returns will be shaped less by fund selection than by the behaviours your platform makes easy or hard.*

This chapter is not about endorsing specific platforms. The market changes, business models evolve, and new entrants appear constantly. Rather, it is a call for *alignment*—between your goals and your tools. A platform is not just a conduit. It is a context. And context always wins. If you want to be a long-term, low-cost, disciplined investor, then choose a platform that makes those traits frictionless. Don't rely on willpower to resist the wrong features. Eliminate them. Don't assume you'll rise above the design. Design for who you are—and for who you're becoming.

Ultimately, the best platform is the one that disappears. That fades into the background of your financial life. That holds your assets securely, executes your instructions reliably, and otherwise leaves you alone. You do not want a platform that teaches you to obsess. You want one that teaches you to *detach*. Because the real work of investing happens away from screens—in habits, in patience, in restraint. Technology should serve that reality. Not distract from it. Choose with care.

The First Purchase: A Ritual of Commitment

There is a curious paradox at the heart of modern investing: with a few taps on a screen, you can allocate capital across the entire global economy. The act is technically trivial. But for the thoughtful investor, placing that first trade is anything but mundane. It represents a commitment—a psychological crossing from theory into practice, from passivity to agency. The screen may look like any other digital interface, but behind it lies an irreversible act of alignment: with one's goals, values, and expectations of the future. For all its procedural simplicity, buying your first ETF marks the beginning of a new intellectual and emotional contract with money.

Before we even reach the transaction itself, there's the prelude—the hours, weeks, or months spent researching, doubting, validating, comparing. New investors often overprepare for their first purchase, obsessing over timing, price, and whether this is "the best possible" entry point. But the truth is that no amount of reading can fully substitute for action. It is only once capital is deployed—however modest the amount—that you start experiencing the real education investing offers. *Markets reward discipline, not theory*. Your learning compounds from practice, not speculation.

Mechanically, placing a trade is now frictionless. Log into your chosen platform. Navigate to the ETF's page—perhaps it's a broad index like the Vanguard FTSE Global All Cap or an S&P 500 tracker like iShares IVV. Select 'Buy'. Choose the amount—either in shares or currency value. Pick an order type: market order if you want immediate execution at the next available price, or limit order if you're willing to wait for a specific price. Confirm, execute. That's it. The trade settles within a couple of business days. Your money has become equity. You are, in every practical sense, an investor.

But this sequence masks the deeper significance of the moment. That first click initiates a shift in identity. You are no longer merely a saver or an observer. You are a participant in the global capital markets. You've joined the ecosystem of ownership, trusting that over time, human ingenuity, enterprise, and capital will reward your risk with return. The decision is not just financial—it is philosophical. It expresses belief in the future, in compounding, in the value of patience. *A single ETF share, held thoughtfully, can be more radical than any tweet, blog post, or debate.*

Yet this commitment carries with it a set of silent emotional challenges. The days following a first purchase are often filled with unease. Did I buy at the top? Should I have waited? What if the price drops tomorrow? These are entirely natural reactions. They stem not from poor reasoning, but from unfamiliarity with volatility. Price movement feels different when it's your money in play. Before the purchase, volatility is abstract. After it, it's visceral. This discomfort is not a sign you've erred—it's a sign you've started. The first purchase introduces you to the emotional terrain you'll need to master.

To mitigate this psychological turbulence, many seasoned investors recommend starting with a modest allocation—an amount small enough to observe without panic, but large enough to feel real. This "toe in the water" strategy builds comfort incrementally. It transforms the unknown into the familiar. As your confidence grows, so does your capital. Dollar-cost averaging—a process covered in the next section—extends this philosophy into a disciplined schedule. But that first trade, however small, does something no plan or projection can: it begins the process of habituation.

One of the most underrated benefits of the first purchase is that it forces clarity. When real money is at stake, all the noise—theorising, procrastination, overthinking—gives way to action. The ETF you choose for your first trade becomes, in some ways, your anchor. It defines your reference point, your starting line. Whether it's a total world fund, a national index, or a sector-specific exposure, the choice sets a precedent. Future decisions will be informed by how this choice performs—not just financially, but psychologically. Did it make you anxious or calm? Did it spark interest or fatigue? These meta-responses are as important as the return figures themselves.

But there is also a trap hidden here: overpersonalisation. New investors often become overly attached to their first ETF, mistaking familiarity for superiority. This emotional imprint can skew judgement. Just because it was your first doesn't mean it should be your only or even your best. A good investor learns to update their assumptions without abandoning their discipline. The first purchase is foundational, not final. It is a point of departure, not a doctrine.

Critically, the act of buying something—anything—counters a pervasive myth: that investing is only for experts. The moment you complete your first ETF purchase, you discover the myth's absurdity. You didn't need an economics degree. You didn't need to forecast GDP. You needed only clarity, intention, and follow-through. This demystification is liberating. It reframes investing not as a high-stakes gamble, but as an accessible, repeatable behaviour. The financial industry benefits when investing feels intimidating. But your future benefits when it becomes *routine.*

The ritual aspect of this act should not be underestimated. Every investor remembers their first trade—not for the fund itself, but for the psychological bridge it helped them cross. There is a reason why seasoned investors speak of "entering the markets" rather than merely opening an account. It's not about the mechanics. It's about the mindset. And like all rituals, the first purchase should be done deliberately. Not recklessly, not flippantly, but with a sense of purpose. It marks the beginning of a long conversation between your values and your volatility tolerance.

There's also a broader cultural dimension to this moment. In an age of distraction, cynicism, and short-termism, committing capital to a long-term investment is a quiet act of optimism. It says: I believe time, not timing, is the lever of wealth. It says: I prefer participation over perfection. It says: I am willing to start, even without certainty. These are not just investment principles—they are character traits. And they get stronger with use.

Finally, we should recognise that this first purchase is not merely about money. It's about agency. It's about taking control of your financial story, no matter how modest the starting sum. It's about turning intention into motion. In behavioural finance, this is known as the action-intention gap—and the best way to close it is to *start.* Not to wait for a perfect moment or perfect knowledge. Just start. Buy one share of a diversified, low-cost ETF. Make it yours. Sit with it. Watch how your thoughts change. Watch how your awareness expands. You have moved from sideline to field. The game is now real. And you are playing it—not for adrenaline, but for accumulation.

This chapter does not glorify the act of trading. Quite the opposite—it elevates the act of restraint, discipline, and intelligent participation. The first ETF you buy will not make you rich. But it will make you an investor. And that identity, forged through one clear decision, is the cornerstone of everything that follows.

Dollar-Cost Averaging: Habit Over Hype

The most effective investment strategy for the vast majority of people has little to do with timing, predictions, or market sentiment. It has everything to do with showing up consistently. Dollar-cost averaging (DCA) is deceptively simple: invest a fixed amount at regular intervals, regardless of market conditions. Yet beneath its simplicity lies a profound set of benefits that reach beyond spreadsheets and into psychology, behavioural finance, and long-term wealth resilience. DCA is not a trick or a tactic. It's a discipline system—*a mechanism to separate action from emotion* and investing from impulsivity.

Most investment advice fails because it assumes a rational actor. But investors are human. They chase highs, flee from lows, second-guess even their most reasoned plans. DCA addresses this not by teaching people to become perfectly rational, but by making rationality automatic. It removes the paralysis of choice. You don't have to guess whether today is a good time to buy. You just invest—weekly, fortnightly, or monthly—on a schedule you've committed to in advance. By making the behaviour repeatable, you make the outcome reliable.

Critics of DCA often argue that it underperforms lump-sum investing in rising markets. Statistically, they're correct: if you had a large amount of capital ready to deploy and perfect knowledge of a bull market, investing all at once would yield higher returns. But that's not the context in which most investors operate. Most people build wealth from regular income, not windfalls. They earn monthly, save monthly, and can only invest monthly. For them, the relevant comparison isn't between DCA and lump-sum—it's between DCA and inconsistency. And measured against emotional whiplash, hesitation, or missed opportunities, *DCA delivers the better behavioural yield.*

Beyond performance metrics, the psychological edge is underappreciated. Volatility is easier to stomach when you're buying through it. When markets dip, your same monthly contribution buys more units—something that feels proactive rather than punishing. This reframing turns downturns into opportunity. The long-term investor no longer fears red days; they learn to welcome them as periods of greater value. Over time, this mental model shift rewires how one relates to risk. The market becomes less a battleground and more a mechanism—volatile, yes, but exploitable through habit.

Consider the real-world applications: a 32-year-old professional earning a stable income decides to invest £500 monthly into a global equity ETF. She sets up an automatic transfer through her brokerage platform, aligned with her payday. Rain or shine, bull or bear, her capital gets deployed on schedule. There is no decision fatigue, no temptation to wait for a "better time." After five years, she's contributed £30,000. Depending on market performance, she may have more or less than that in value—but critically, *she has trained a muscle.* Investing is no longer an aspirational task—it's part of her life rhythm, as habitual as brushing teeth or paying the mortgage.

A key insight here is that financial success often flows from structural design, not situational brilliance. People overrate the importance of great decisions and underrate the power of good defaults. DCA is the ultimate default. It systematises what otherwise requires constant vigilance. And in doing so, it creates a stable base upon which more nuanced strategies—like rebalancing, tax-loss harvesting, or adding satellite positions—can rest. *Without a stable core, complexity becomes fragility.*

Still, DCA is not without nuance. For it to work optimally, certain principles must be observed. First, the assets chosen must be appropriate for long-term compounding. Applying DCA to speculative or short-term vehicles can backfire; it's not a magical hedge against bad investments. Second, the schedule must be realistic and sustainable. Overcommitting and pulling back later defeats the purpose. It's better to start modestly and grow with confidence than to rush and retreat. Third, automation should be coupled with periodic reflection. Set-it-and-forget-it doesn't mean ignore-it-forever. Quarterly or annual reviews ensure alignment with goals, risk tolerance, and life changes.

There's also a powerful emotional component to automating your contributions: it helps decouple identity from short-term market outcomes. When you manually execute every trade, each decision feels personal. If your purchase is followed by a dip, you feel foolish. If prices rise, you feel clever. This fragile ego loop increases your exposure to overreaction. But with DCA, you mute this noise. You become a process-oriented investor—focused less on being right and more on being regular. This posture has profound implications. *Discipline, not genius, is the edge that compounds.*

Many of history's most successful investors—from John Bogle to Jack Meyer—have emphasised repeatable process over tactical brilliance. What DCA offers is not superior returns in every market, but a superior behavioural framework in all markets. It allows ordinary investors to harness the same consistency that endowments, pensions, and sovereign wealth funds institutionalise. Whether you're investing £100 a month or £10,000, the mindset is the same: act reliably, not reactively.

Some critics argue that DCA delays exposure to the market and thus can miss out on time in the market—especially when deployed in a context of one-off lump sums. This is a valid objection in specific cases. For investors sitting on a large inheritance or bonus, a thoughtful blend of partial lump-sum and partial DCA might be more appropriate. But for wage earners and early accumulators—the backbone of the global investing population—the delayed exposure critique is largely irrelevant. Their capital arrives over time, so DCA isn't a compromise—it's a conduit.

It's also worth addressing the idea that DCA is "boring." This critique, often levied by those chasing high-beta strategies, misunderstands the nature of compounding. *Wealth is built not through adrenaline, but through accumulation.* The monthly contribution doesn't need to thrill you. It needs to be there. Like soil and sunlight, its value emerges not in a single day, but across many seasons. The more attention we give to short-term stimulation, the less we give to long-term structure. DCA is boring by design—and powerful because of it.

At a practical level, choosing your DCA schedule should reflect your cash flow cadence. Monthly is most common, as it aligns with payroll. But bi-weekly or even weekly options may enhance discipline for those with variable income or less impulse control. The key is predictability. Your DCA process should be immune to mood, media, or momentum. It should operate like a metronome—steady, unperturbed, indifferent to narrative. Over time, this cadence becomes a signal to yourself: I am building something, regardless of noise.

In aggregate, DCA turns investing from an episodic act into a lifestyle. It aligns finance with habit, automation with agency. It's not just about smoothing volatility, although it does. It's about smoothing emotion—blunting the twin temptations of panic and greed. Most investors don't fail because they pick the wrong assets. They fail because they abandon the right ones too early. DCA doesn't eliminate risk, but it radically reduces the behavioural failure rate.

Ultimately, dollar-cost averaging is not a strategy for the impatient. It is a system for the consistent. It doesn't appeal to those chasing the next 10x return. It appeals to those who understand that time is the true multiplier. In that sense, DCA is more than a tactic—it is a posture, a philosophy of engagement. You don't invest because the market is up or down. You invest because it's the first Friday of the month. *And that ritual, repeated enough times, becomes a compound habit—one that pays dividends far beyond price charts.*

When to Sell (and When Not To)

Buying gets the attention, but selling defines the outcome. What you own is only as valuable as your ability to hold—or exit—with discipline. Yet selling remains one of the least taught, most emotionally fraught aspects of investing. Too often, investors sell for the wrong reasons: panic, impatience, boredom, headlines, or fleeting regrets. They abandon long-term positions not because the thesis broke, but because their conviction wavered. *The challenge is not knowing when to sell; it's knowing when not to.*

The fundamental error most investors make is mistaking discomfort for risk. A market correction, a disappointing quarterly report, or political turbulence prompts action—not always because the data justifies it, but because the feeling does. Selling, in this sense, is often a coping mechanism. It offers relief, but rarely reward. If buying is an expression of belief, selling should be an act of reasoned revision. The problem is that most investors reverse the two: they buy emotionally and sell reactively.

A more principled approach begins with understanding the primary function of selling within a portfolio. It should not be an impulsive exit, but a deliberate reallocation. You are not fleeing an asset; you are reallocating capital to a higher-conviction use. That shift may be from equities to bonds, from developed markets to emerging, or from a risky satellite holding back into a core ETF. But in each case, the act of selling should be tethered to a *strategic purpose*—not sentiment.

There are, of course, legitimate reasons to sell. Life changes often justify shifts in asset allocation. Retiring individuals may need to reduce equity exposure to fund spending. A young investor may switch funds to improve global diversification. Regulatory or tax changes can also drive portfolio adjustments. But the thread running through all sound exits is intentionality. The investor has thought about the *why*, not just the *when*.

Let's be precise. Selling because a stock or fund has gone up significantly is not, by itself, a reason to sell. Neither is a short-term dip. A 15% drawdown in a global equity ETF, while uncomfortable, is not rare. It is expected. The act of investing is an acceptance of such volatility. Selling during that period typically locks in losses—and denies you the rebound. Historically, most of the market's best days cluster around its worst. If you're out during the lows, you're likely out during the highs too. *Impatience, not poor selection, often causes underperformance.*

Real-world case studies reinforce this. During the COVID-19 market crash in March 2020, many retail investors sold their ETF holdings at a loss. But those who stayed invested or even added to their positions saw full recoveries within months. The pain of watching prices fall is undeniable. But those who built their portfolios with a long-term thesis and respected it through the noise came out ahead. Their strength was not foresight—it was staying power.

Another peril is selling in response to macroeconomic shifts that are already priced in. By the time inflation is in the headlines or interest rates are being raised, markets have likely adjusted. Reacting to news can mean acting on stale information. A better approach is to stress-test your portfolio in advance. Ask: if inflation rises, if a recession hits, if currency weakens—how will my holdings behave? If the answer is unacceptable, make structural changes proactively. Selling in panic is costly; rebalancing with foresight is prudent.

It's also worth addressing the fallacy of breakeven bias. Investors often hold losing positions not because they believe in their recovery, but because they want to "get back to even." This is emotionally understandable but financially irrational. The market does not owe you a rebound. What matters is expected future return. If you wouldn't buy the asset today, you shouldn't hold it. Selling should be tied to forward-looking rationale, not backward-looking hope.

The inverse mistake is selling winners too early. This behaviour—often driven by the urge to "lock in gains"—can truncate compounding. Some of the best-performing assets take years to realise their potential. Selling a high-quality fund or ETF after a 20% gain, when the underlying trend remains intact, may be satisfying in the moment but damaging long term. One must learn to distinguish between cyclical fluctuations and structural shifts. *The goal is not to sell because it went up—it's to sell because your reason for owning it no longer holds.*

Principled selling requires a framework. A strong starting point is to ask yourself three questions before executing a sell order:

1. Has the investment's fundamental thesis changed?
2. Have your personal circumstances or goals changed?
3. Is there a clearly superior alternative for the capital?

If none of these apply, hesitation is often wise. The best investors are not the most active—they are the most discerning. They understand that activity is not synonymous with progress. A good portfolio, like a good garden, grows best with occasional pruning—not constant replanting.

It is equally essential to understand the behavioural traps around selling. Loss aversion, recency bias, and confirmation bias all skew decision-making. Investors are more sensitive to losses than gains. They overreact to recent news. They seek information that affirms their existing fears. These cognitive errors make it far more likely that a sell will be poorly timed. Embedding rules in your investing process—such as "never sell on a red day" or "only rebalance once per quarter"—can create guardrails against emotional reaction.

The use of automation can also help. Rebalancing algorithms, percentage-based asset allocation rules, and pre-set target ranges reduce the need for gut-based selling. For instance, if your equity exposure grows beyond your intended 70%, an automatic rebalance trims it—not because you're scared, but because your plan demands it. *Systematised discipline outperforms discretionary interference.* In practice, this means building an architecture of decisions in advance, so future actions don't rely on your mood.

For those who feel compelled to sell in periods of stress, an alternative is to write down the reason—then wait 48 hours. Often, the emotional charge fades. You return to the decision with clearer eyes. If the rationale still holds, proceed. If not, you've dodged a costly mistake. This pause-and-reflect habit is surprisingly powerful. It transforms reaction into revision.

Selling should never be about chasing peaks or timing troughs. The goal is not perfection—it's alignment. Sell when the asset no longer aligns with your plan. Sell when your goals evolve. Sell when the position has become unreasonably concentrated. But do not sell because others are. Do not sell because of headlines. And do not sell because doing nothing feels too passive.

To be clear, some portfolios require deliberate trimming. A high-conviction satellite fund that has grown to dominate your allocation may need to be pared back to preserve balance. A thematic ETF that no longer fits your macro view should be exited. Tax planning may warrant harvesting capital losses at year-end. These are rational, plan-driven actions. What must be avoided is the kind of selling that masquerades as action but is really avoidance: avoidance of discomfort, of ambiguity, of patience.

In the end, the mark of a seasoned investor is not how often they act—but how well they refrain. Selling is not failure; it's a tool. Like any tool, it must be used intentionally, not impulsively. The investor who sells with principle protects their future returns. The one who sells reactively undermines them. *To hold is to believe. To sell is to revise. The strength lies in knowing when each is required—and having the clarity to choose deliberately.*

Chapter 9
Measuring What Matters

Most investors fixate on returns because they are the most conspicuous measure. Bold numbers, jagged charts, rankings splashed across financial newspapers—all of it conspires to keep our gaze glued to performance. Yet performance, narrowly understood as returns over time, is not synonymous with progress. And progress—let's be candid—is the real aim: achieving goals with assurance, clarity, and minimal regret. To gauge what truly matters, one must look beyond the gleaming figures.

The issue is not that returns are irrelevant; it's that they are partial, often misleading. Focusing on them alone is akin to judging a car solely by its top speed: essential qualities—risk, reliability, comfort—get pushed aside in pursuit of a single statistic. In investing, the overlooked variables include volatility, drawdowns, risk-adjusted returns, tracking error, and, most crucially, peace of mind. The discerning investor does not merely chase returns—they evaluate the integrity of the journey producing them.

Picture two portfolios: one yielding 8% annually but subject to wild swings—a 40% drawdown here, a jarring quarterly drop there—and another offering 6% with steady, predictable growth. Most investors, particularly those funding retirement, education, or long-term family plans, would gravitate toward the latter. Yet human psychology, peer influence, and reductive reporting often convince people that the first is superior. The result? Unnecessary risk, ill-timed sales, and emotional turbulence that erodes discipline.

Risk-adjusted return, though frequently underestimated, is a vital compass. Metrics like the Sharpe or Sortino ratios provide ways to weigh performance against volatility and downside exposure. More importantly, these tools illuminate personal investment strategy. Are the returns truly earned, or merely endured? The answers are not theoretical—they form the bedrock of prudent, sustainable investing.

Drawdowns tell a story that returns cannot. The eye may follow the upward trajectory, but few anticipate the dips that accompany it. A temporary loss of 30% in a portfolio can shake even seasoned investors. Most people only discover their real tolerance for risk when confronted with it. Studying historical drawdowns—whether in ETFs or simple "lazy" portfolios—is not mere technicality; it is psychological preparation. Successful investing is not about avoiding discomfort, but understanding it—its scope, its likelihood, and your capacity to endure it.

Then there is volatility: those daily oscillations that, while trivial in the long run, can provoke poor decisions. A 2% market dip may be statistically normal, yet emotionally, it can spark panic. Volatility itself is benign; our reactions are not. Grasping this distinction is not simply intellectual; it must be internalised. Acceptance and preparedness are what allow investors to maintain course.

Lurking beyond these measures is a subtler hazard: tracking error. Essentially, it is the divergence of a portfolio's returns from a benchmark. While the concept sounds arcane, its emotional weight is considerable. A portfolio slightly underperforming the S&P 500—yet safer or better aligned with personal goals—can feel like failure if judged against the wrong metric. Succumbing to the allure of chasing today's "winners" can destabilise long-term progress. Embracing intentional tracking error is a sign of maturity: it is not about beating the index, but about fulfilling your mandate.

To determine what matters, one must first define what matters personally. This demands self-awareness alongside financial knowledge. Journaling, surprisingly, is invaluable here. Recording the rationale behind each investment, reactions to market events, and reflections on outcomes creates a living archive of decision-making. Over time, patterns emerge: moments of reactivity, of prudence, of adherence to or abandonment of strategy. No app or automated platform can replicate this insight. It is discipline and reward intertwined.

The most effective journals are concise: a note like, "Bought global equity ETF for long-term growth potential; expect to hold through volatility," can prevent premature exits during downturns months later. The journal's purpose is not to impress; it is to anchor. Clarity accumulates, but only if captured in the moment.

Finally, we must rethink success. Markets measure themselves with indices; investors should not. Anchoring self-assessment to index levels is as absurd as defining self-worth by the weather. Real progress is personal: funding a child's education, reaching a comfortable retirement, clearing a mortgage, taking a sabbatical. The market exists to serve these ends—not to overshadow them.

A portfolio trailing the S&P 500 by 1% annually but enabling restful sleep, continued investment, and goal attainment is performing admirably. Achieving this mindset requires disentangling ego from outcome, resisting social comparison, media noise, and the fleeting thrill of account fluctuations. Standards must be personal, not performative.

Measuring what matters is not about mastering spreadsheets. It is about refining the feedback loop that guides investment decisions. When we evaluate our financial life through enduring utility rather than immediate visibility, we construct a resilient system capable of weathering all seasons. Smarter metrics, attention to hidden distortions, and disciplined reflection transform not just portfolios, but the investors themselves.

Because competent investors know what they own; great investors understand why it matters.

"Returns Are Not Everything":

If there is one idea that dominates most casual investing conversations—and misleads more investors than it guides—it is this: the notion that the return number, standing tall and proud at the end of a chart or on a performance page, tells the whole story. It does not. Returns are merely the outcome of a process. To judge an investment—or a portfolio—by returns alone is akin to evaluating a novel by its page count. What matters more is *how* those returns were achieved: the risks endured, the volatility accepted, the mental strain weathered, and the sustainability of the strategy itself.

The allure of performance-chasing is ancient and persistent. Every generation of investors eventually rediscovers that past returns are not predictive, and that strategies boasting the highest historical gains often carry hidden fragilities. Yet the cycle repeats because returns are easy to measure, emotionally compelling, and often dressed in the authority of numbers. But mature investing demands a deeper lens—one that examines *risk-adjusted returns*, *maximum drawdowns*, *volatility profiles*, and, most critically, *the investor's capacity to remain invested* through all conditions.

Risk-adjusted return is a deceptively simple concept: how much reward did the investor receive per unit of risk taken? Yet this idea contains multitudes. A fund returning 10% annually may seem superior to one returning 8%, until one realises that the first fund routinely loses 30% in down years, while the second rarely drops more than 10%. Which would you hold through a crisis? Which would you continue contributing to when the headlines are filled with panic? *Sharpe ratio*, *Sortino ratio*, and *standard deviation* are not academic abstractions—they are tools that help the thoughtful investor align returns with the actual emotional and financial costs of attaining them.

Consider the behaviour of two hypothetical portfolios from 2007 to 2022. The first, an aggressive global equity strategy, delivered a stellar average annual return of 9.5%—but with a gut-wrenching 55% drawdown during the 2008 financial crisis. The second, a balanced allocation of 60% equities and 40% bonds, returned only 7% per year—but never experienced a drawdown worse than 20%. Which strategy is superior? From a spreadsheet perspective, the aggressive portfolio wins. But for a real-world investor trying to fund retirement, raise children, or sleep at night during a crisis, the balanced portfolio is often the wiser path. *The best investment strategy is not the one with the highest returns—it is the one you can actually stick with.*

Drawdowns, the peak-to-trough declines that occur within any investment strategy, reveal more than volatility—they expose vulnerability. A deep drawdown does not merely hurt a portfolio; it tests the conviction and resilience of the investor behind it. And while market history tells us that most portfolios recover in time, investor behaviour often breaks long before the market does. The consequence is rarely just financial; it is psychological. Selling at the bottom out of panic, switching to cash "until things stabilise," or chasing the next hot fund after a recovery has begun—these behaviours stem from underestimating *the emotional tax* of volatility and overestimating one's risk tolerance.

Volatility itself is another misunderstood metric. Most investors imagine it as something to be endured or avoided. But volatility, properly understood, is not simply the frequency of price movements—it is a measure of uncertainty, of how widely a portfolio's value can swing over a given period. Some volatility is necessary; it is the price of entry into the world of equities and long-term growth. But excessive volatility, particularly when coupled with leverage or concentration, can make even the most promising portfolio *unlivable.* A high-return strategy that causes sleepless nights, compulsive checking of account balances, or second-guessing in every downturn is, ultimately, self-defeating. The portfolio may survive, but the investor may not.

This brings us to a rarely discussed but foundational dimension of investment evaluation: *peace of mind.* While intangible, it is perhaps the most consequential performance metric of all. A portfolio that aligns with one's values, risk appetite, and life goals—and that allows one to live their life without chronic anxiety about the markets—is often underrated in performance tables but profoundly valuable in real terms. Peace of mind is not the enemy of ambition; it is the enabler of consistency. The investor who can commit to a steady strategy for decades will, over time, outperform the one who jumps between extremes—even if the latter appears, on paper, more "optimised."

The industry often promotes annualised returns as the gold standard of comparison. But annualised returns can obscure more than they reveal. Two funds with identical 10-year annualised returns may have radically different journeys: one smooth and consistent, the other marked by huge swings and prolonged periods of underperformance. The question is not just "What did the fund earn?" but also "*What did the investor have to go through to earn it?*" and "*Could they realistically have stayed invested throughout that journey?*"

It is here that investor psychology meets portfolio construction. A strategy's theoretical performance matters far less than the investor's *behavioural ability* to endure its ups and downs. This is why diversification is not merely about reducing volatility on a spreadsheet; it is about reducing *behavioural volatility*—the tendency to make destructive decisions at precisely the wrong times. A portfolio that slightly underperforms the market, but keeps the investor invested through thick and thin, is often far superior to one that dazzles but demands nerves of steel.

Moreover, portfolios should be measured not only against abstract benchmarks but against *personal benchmarks*. A retiree drawing income from a conservative allocation may never match the S&P 500—but if their portfolio supports their lifestyle reliably and sustainably, they are achieving success. Likewise, a young professional saving aggressively may prioritise accumulation over optimisation, accepting some volatility in exchange for long-term wealth-building. *Success in investing is always context-dependent. Metrics must reflect the investor's purpose, not someone else's.*

This reframing demands new habits. Investors must look beyond "What did I earn this year?" and ask instead, "*Did I take the right risks for the right reasons?*" "*Did my strategy behave as expected during market stress?*" "*Am I still confident in my process, or am I reacting to noise?*" This is where *risk-adjusted metrics* regain their power—not as mathematical curiosities but as reflections of the investor's ability to act rationally across time.

Take, for example, the concept of the *Sortino ratio*, which refines the Sharpe ratio by penalising only downside volatility. This matters because upside volatility rarely disturbs investors—only the downside does. Likewise, *maximum drawdown* offers a cleaner view into the worst-case scenario a portfolio has endured. These are not academic details; they are survival guides. They tell investors what kind of stress they are likely to endure—not in theory, but in lived experience.

Over time, the wisdom of prioritising resilience over returns becomes clear. The investor who understands this early—and structures their portfolio accordingly—builds not only wealth, but confidence, clarity, and calm. Their decisions are not driven by envy of others' returns or the latest headlines, but by alignment with their own goals and limits.

The takeaway is radical in its simplicity: *Returns matter, but they do not matter most.* The true performance of a portfolio is measured not by what it earns in ideal conditions, but by how it holds up under pressure, how well it fits the life of its owner, and how faithfully it supports the investor in staying the course. In that light, the most important question becomes not "What was the return?" but "*Was it worth it?*"

"The Silent Power of Tracking Error":

Investors often believe they are making rational decisions. They compare performance against a benchmark—perhaps the S&P 500, a global equity index, or a blended portfolio—and expect that small deviations are inconsequential. But what appears as a minor gap in short-term results can mask profound long-term divergences. *Tracking error*, the difference between a portfolio's return and that of its benchmark, may seem like a technical detail, but over decades, it holds transformative—and often destructive—power over investor outcomes. And perhaps more importantly, over investor behaviour.

The promise of index investing lies in its elegant simplicity: own the market, accept market returns, and avoid unnecessary costs. It's a powerful proposition. Yet many investors who claim to follow this discipline stray quietly from its core. A portfolio that mimics an index "most of the time" but not all the time can still experience substantial differences in outcome—and behaviour—when those deviations add up or coincide with periods of stress. *Even a small tracking error, compounded by misaligned expectations, can trigger disillusionment, regret, or abandonment of an otherwise sound strategy.*

Consider the investor who builds what they believe is a globally diversified ETF portfolio. Their holdings include a mix of U.S. equities, developed markets, and some exposure to emerging economies. But they overweight technology stocks slightly, hold an actively managed dividend fund, and exclude small caps due to perceived risk. On paper, they're 90% aligned with a global benchmark like the MSCI ACWI. But that 10% difference—repeated annually, rebalanced imperfectly, or skewed during market extremes—creates an accumulating divergence. Over five years, they may trail the benchmark by 50 to 100 basis points annually. Over 20 years, that lag compounds into a significant shortfall. *The gap between expectation and reality, more than the actual return, becomes the source of disappointment.*

Tracking error is not merely about numbers—it's about *narrative discipline.* Investors often adopt a benchmark mentally, even if not formally. They measure progress, judge advisors, and make allocation decisions through the lens of what the "market" did. But unless their portfolio truly mirrors that benchmark in composition, weightings, and risk factors, any such comparison is not only flawed—it is misleading. A portfolio cannot be 80% benchmark and 20% opinion without inviting confusion. *Half-fidelity to an index invites full exposure to behavioural error.*

The psychology becomes especially fragile during underperformance. Suppose an investor has deviated from the benchmark—perhaps by tilting toward value stocks, or allocating to gold, or incorporating tactical shifts based on macro forecasts. If those moves underperform, and the investor sees their strategy lag the market during strong years, frustration mounts. They may question their process, second-guess their decisions, or abandon the strategy altogether. But the deeper error was not the deviation itself—it was *believing they were tracking the benchmark when they were not.*

Moreover, tracking error is often amplified by fees, frictions, and timing misjudgements. A portfolio with modest deviation from an index might still incur higher transaction costs or inefficiencies if built through multiple overlapping ETFs. Currency fluctuations, dividend handling, and tax treatment can introduce further distortion. The result is that the investor's experience diverges not only in return but also in *emotional texture*—more surprises, more corrections, and more uncertainty. These are not statistical abstractions; they are real triggers for impulsive decisions.

This is why it's critical to be intellectually honest about the strategy you are actually implementing. If you are not fully tracking an index, you must not measure yourself against it—or expect identical outcomes. The discipline of passive investing only works if the implementation is faithful. The further one drifts from that core, the more they must own the consequences—and the complexity.

There is also a subtle asymmetry at play. When tracking error leads to outperformance, investors tend to attribute it to skill. When it leads to underperformance, they blame the market or the tools. This asymmetry fuels narrative distortion. Investors begin to tinker, believing they can capture alpha on top of the beta they claim to follow. But this half-active, half-passive approach is rarely repeatable. It injects unnecessary variability into outcomes and undermines the key advantage of index investing: *predictability and consistency.*

Another dimension of tracking error is behavioural benchmarking. Many investors do not compare themselves to a broad market index but to the returns of friends, peers, or prominent financial figures. This social benchmarking is deeply corrosive. It encourages reactive behaviour and shifts focus from *process* to *performance.* An investor with a well-designed, risk-aligned portfolio may feel inadequate if they underperform a trend-driven allocation that surged in a given year. But markets mean-revert; discipline does not. The pursuit of short-term alignment with what's "winning now" often leads to long-term regret.

We must also consider the institutional context. Pension funds, endowments, and large asset managers track performance meticulously against benchmarks. But many have broader mandates—liability matching, capital preservation, income generation. Even here, tracking error has political consequences: an investment committee underperforms the benchmark for three consecutive years and faces pressure to change managers or strategy. The same dynamic plays out in personal portfolios, though the consequences are internalised. *Tracking error, when misunderstood, becomes a psychological landmine.*

So what truly matters over decades? Not perfect alignment with an index, but *consistency of purpose, coherence of strategy, and clarity of expectations.* If you choose to track an index, do it precisely and systematically. If you choose to deviate, acknowledge it upfront and set new benchmarks that reflect your strategy honestly. This transparency—both internal and external—is the antidote to tracking error's corrosive effects.

It is worth remembering that tracking error, by itself, is not inherently bad. Many strategies that outperform over time do so because they deviate meaningfully from a benchmark. Factor tilts, value investing, quality screens, and ESG overlays all introduce tracking error. But such strategies require *conviction, time horizon, and emotional discipline.* Without these, the short-term discomfort of deviation will overpower the long-term potential of outperformance.

Investors must also guard against what might be called *tracking illusion*—the belief that an ETF or fund is benchmark-aligned because it carries a familiar label or index name. Not all S&P 500 funds are created equal. Differences in replication strategy, fee structure, tax efficiency, or currency hedging can create material differences in return. Similarly, "global equity" ETFs may be heavily weighted toward the United States or specific sectors. It is not enough to know the name—you must understand the composition.

Ultimately, tracking error invites us to think more deeply about alignment—between our strategy and our goals, our benchmarks and our beliefs, our expectations and our execution. It challenges us to ask: *What am I truly measuring myself against? And is that a fair, accurate, and meaningful reference point for my actual portfolio and my actual life?*

The investors who understand this will not be swayed by transient underperformance or overconfidence in momentary success. They will measure progress not by proximity to a benchmark, but by fidelity to a thoughtful process. They will resist the temptation to chase the market and embrace the stability of a well-defined strategy. And in doing so, they will find that over decades, tracking error matters—not because of a few missed percentage points, but because of what it reveals about the investor's clarity, discipline, and ultimate success.

Journaling Your Investment Thinking:

Every investor has intentions. Fewer record them. Fewer still revisit them with honesty. And yet, the distance between an average investor and a disciplined one is often not access to information or a better model—it's documentation. *A written investment journal is not an administrative exercise; it's an intellectual anchor.* It forces coherence where memory fails, filters emotion, and builds a private compendium of thought patterns—exactly the raw material most crucial for long-term learning.

The investing world celebrates backtests, track records, and ratios. But it tends to neglect introspection. An ETF portfolio, by design, may appear low-maintenance and objective. But even the most passive strategy is carried out by a human being—one who checks the markets during volatile weeks, reads headlines, and wrestles with uncertainty. That human is not fixed in temperament. Their decisions, even if framed as systematic, are subject to drift. And without a written trace of what they believed, feared, or rationalised at a given moment, their own evolution becomes unreadable.

This is why investment journaling matters. Not as a diary of prices, but as a continuous narrative of decision-making. *A journal creates a timestamped mirror: what did you expect, and why? What alternatives did you reject, and on what grounds? What was your emotional state when the trade was placed, or when it wasn't?* These are the data points of personal investing history. And when aggregated across months or years, they yield a sharper understanding than any chart can offer.

The most effective investors are rarely those with the most aggressive strategies. They are those who consistently align their behaviour with a deliberate philosophy. But alignment is not accidental—it is tracked, tested, and tuned. A journal is how that tuning occurs. When the market corrects sharply and panic tempts a deviation from plan, rereading your own prior entries—written in calmer times—can provide a stabilising reference. When you are tempted to chase a hot sector or abandon a lagging asset class, a record of past enthusiasm (and disappointment) tempers the cycle.

More importantly, a journal enables pattern recognition. You might realise that each time you acted on macro forecasts, you underperformed. Or that your most confident allocations were often poorly timed. These aren't revelations that come from hindsight bias—they come from disciplined documentation. *The goal of journaling is not perfection in forecasting, but precision in self-awareness.*

This isn't a call for elaborate prose. A sentence is often enough. "Bought more global equities despite recent dip; thesis unchanged." Or: "Felt uneasy about rebalancing, delayed decision; need to examine why." What matters is consistency and candour. Over time, even minimal entries form a psychological map—a record not of what the market did, but of how you responded, justified, and reflected.

Crucially, journaling is not about performance attribution. It's about *decision attribution.* A portfolio might go up for the wrong reasons, or down despite solid reasoning. Without a journal, these outcomes blur into noise. But with a journal, you can separate luck from process. You begin to refine your own cognitive filters—not based on dogma, but on evidence from your own lived strategy.

Take, for example, a long-term ETF investor committed to a 70/30 global stock/bond allocation. On paper, the strategy is automated. But over time, real-world complexity creeps in: Should I pause contributions during a recession? Should I switch to inflation-linked bonds? Is now the time to tilt toward emerging markets? Each of these forks presents a psychological challenge. *By recording the question, the reasoning, and the decision—whether action or inaction—the investor constructs a decision tree they can audit later.*

Journaling also forces clarity before execution. Knowing you will have to write down your rationale encourages deeper thinking. It becomes harder to act on vague intuition when you know you'll revisit the logic in six months. The act of anticipating your future self—who will read that entry with the benefit of hindsight—is a powerful check on impulsivity.

There's also a philosophical benefit: journaling builds a more intimate relationship with your strategy. You stop being a passive participant in a market driven by headlines. You become a student of your own convictions. And in doing so, you develop intellectual resilience. *When the market shifts, you don't just react; you compare the new reality against your previous assumptions and calibrate accordingly.*

Some investors may prefer digital tools—apps, spreadsheets, or automated trackers. Others will gravitate toward pen and paper. The medium is secondary. What matters is continuity. And more than that: *privacy.* The journal is not for performance marketing or social validation. It is a private forum where honesty trumps aesthetics. The language can be blunt, the structure informal, but the insights are yours alone.

One counterargument is that disciplined investing should be boring and mechanical—so why journal something that doesn't change much? The answer is that *the market may be repetitive, but your internal dialogue isn't.* The temptations shift. The macro noise evolves. The life context matures. A 35-year-old investing for early retirement may journal about income optimisation and risk appetite. A 50-year-old may write about capital preservation or college expenses. A retiree may reflect on drawdowns and the fear of depletion. The strategy may be stable—but the context is not static. Journaling captures that evolution.

There's also a strategic feedback loop at play. After five or ten years of consistent journaling, you'll be able to see more than your net worth curve. You'll see your mental frameworks in formation—how you learned, where you faltered, and which instincts proved reliable. This allows you to iterate. Maybe you realise you're consistently overconfident during bull markets. Maybe you see that you're most anxious at market bottoms. These are not personality flaws—they are traits. Once recognised, they can be integrated into how you structure decisions. *Self-knowledge becomes a competitive advantage.*

This reflective posture also helps inoculate against overreaction. When you can say, "I've felt this before, and here's what happened," you build behavioural immunity. This does not mean you become emotionally detached. Rather, you become *emotionally fluent*—able to feel the fear or excitement, but process it with awareness.

In a financial world obsessed with external metrics—Sharpe ratios, alpha, standard deviation—a journal redirects the spotlight inward. It treats investor psychology not as an afterthought, but as a primary data source. And in doing so, it elevates the act of investing from mechanical execution to *deliberate craft.*

There is no single correct way to journal. What matters is that it's authentic, regular, and cumulative. Over time, the discipline of writing creates a second portfolio—not of assets, but of insights. It becomes your most personal financial document—not because of what it says about the market, but because of what it reveals about you.

Milestones Over Markets:

There is a quiet tyranny in financial media: the notion that progress must be measured by market indices. That if the S&P 500 is up, you are winning; and if it's down, something is wrong. For most investors, this framing is not just unhelpful—it's harmful. It shifts attention away from real, lived goals and redirects it toward abstract benchmarks. But investing, for thoughtful individuals, is not a game of outperforming strangers. *It is a personal system of enabling a life you care about.* The metric that matters most is not how your portfolio did relative to the FTSE or MSCI World—it's whether your money is aligned with your milestones.

Milestones are inherently personal. They are not found in spreadsheets or earnings reports; they emerge from context: raising a child, funding a sabbatical, supporting ageing parents, starting a business, reaching partial financial independence, or simply reducing work hours to regain time. None of these objectives require outperforming a benchmark. *They require planning, persistence, and clarity.* But clarity cannot emerge if success is defined by the wrong scoreboard.

Benchmarking against indices may have a place for institutional investors who report to boards and manage public funds. But for individual investors, it often breeds dissatisfaction. Suppose you planned to accumulate £250,000 in 15 years to pay off a mortgage early. If you're on track, it should be a success. But if your portfolio lagged the global equity index by 0.5% this year, should you feel disappointed? The financial industry would suggest yes. Rationally, the answer is no. *Your plan is intact. Your goal is progressing. And the benchmark, in this case, is irrelevant.*

This disconnect matters because misaligned metrics distort behaviour. Investors who focus excessively on market performance often take unnecessary risks to "catch up" with indices. They may chase trends, abandon diversification, or shift strategies mid-cycle. But those who define success by their own milestones tend to be steadier. Their reference point is internal. When the market declines, they ask: has my ability to meet my goal materially changed? If not, they stay the course.

Consider two investors. One checks their net worth monthly against the S&P 500. The other tracks whether their retirement account is on track to replace 70% of income by age 60. The former is likely to experience a rollercoaster of emotions—excitement, anxiety, disappointment—none of which necessarily map to their actual needs. The latter is likely to experience something rarer in investing: *peace of mind.* Because they have reframed performance as progress, not comparison.

Reframing does not mean ignoring numbers. It means choosing the right ones. Risk-adjusted returns, drawdowns, and savings rates are more meaningful than raw performance alone. But even these should be connected to real objectives. For instance, understanding volatility is important not just because it's a technical metric, but because it helps answer a human question: can I stick with this strategy through rough periods? If not, I may need to recalibrate—not to improve returns, but to increase my odds of staying invested.

This reframing also opens up space for more inclusive definitions of success. Traditional financial literature celebrates early retirement, aggressive growth, and beating the market. But what if your goal is to work fewer hours and increase flexibility while maintaining a modest lifestyle? Or to support a dependent without compromising your own financial future? These goals don't always lend themselves to compound-interest projections or bar charts. Yet they are valid, sophisticated objectives that deserve financial strategies of equal nuance.

By tying performance to personal milestones, investors begin to see their money not as a scoreboard, but as a *tool.* This subtle shift can radically alter decision-making. For instance, someone who values stability might accept a slightly lower return for a more predictable portfolio, knowing it supports their milestone of taking a year off work to care for a family member. Another might invest more aggressively early in their career, knowing their real milestone is optionality—not early retirement, but the freedom to change jobs at 45 without panic. *Success, then, becomes about alignment, not optimisation.*

This mindset also promotes more honest planning. When the destination is personal, shortcuts lose their appeal. A speculative bet on cryptocurrency looks less compelling when your milestone is paying for your child's education. Similarly, market downturns become less existential. If you're two years away from a planned sabbatical and markets drop 10%, the right question is not "how did I perform versus the index?" It is: "Can I still take the time off I planned? And if not, what adjustments are within my control?" These are grounded, solvable questions. They anchor the investor in reality.

There is also a broader philosophical implication. Obsession with markets tends to fragment time into quarters, years, and short-term cycles. Milestones stretch time out. They reintroduce patience. When you think in 10- or 20-year arcs—children growing, careers evolving, health changing—the daily market report fades into background noise. This long view is not just healthier; it is more truthful. Most goals worth pursuing exist on a decade scale. Yet most financial media is designed to provoke weekly or monthly anxiety. *Milestone-based thinking immunises you from that churn.*

Critically, this approach makes room for reflection. Rather than asking only "how did my portfolio perform?" it invites the question: "How did my life evolve in relation to my financial intentions?" Maybe you postponed a goal due to family illness. Maybe your values shifted, and the milestone changed. A milestone-based framework is adaptable. It respects the reality that *you will change over time*, and therefore, so will the definition of success.

Some may worry that this perspective encourages complacency—that without market benchmarks, we lose rigour. The opposite is true. Milestone-based investing demands a deeper kind of honesty. It requires you to articulate your priorities, quantify your needs, and design systems that match. That's harder than copying an index or tracking a leaderboard. But it's also more enduring. Because at the end of a 30-year investment career, it is not the number on your brokerage statement that matters most. It is whether the money helped build the life you wanted.

Redefining success this way also helps in communication—especially for couples or families. Discussing market returns often sparks disagreement or disengagement. Discussing milestones—"When can we reduce our workload?" "When do we want to be debt-free?"—creates alignment. It turns investing into a shared language of priorities. And it places agency where it belongs: not in external benchmarks, but in intentional choices.

This chapter does not dismiss performance. It contextualises it. A healthy portfolio still needs to grow. But growth is not the only metric, nor always the most important one. Stability, adaptability, liquidity, and simplicity are equally valid, depending on what you are optimising for. And that is the key: *you must define what you are optimising for—before the market defines it for you.*

Ultimately, tying financial progress to personal milestones restores meaning to the act of investing. It reminds us that capital is not an end in itself, but a means. That portfolios are not playgrounds for speculation, but engines of support for a life of greater autonomy. And that success, if it is to be sustainable, must be self-defined—measured not against indices, but against the milestones that mark a life well lived.

Chapter 10
Beyond the Money: Investing as a Way of Being

Most investment guides pile on more numbers. This one takes a pause—for perspective. Not another chart, not another benchmark, but a confrontation with the question few investors are encouraged to ask: what is all this for? After navigating ETFs, asset allocation, global diversification, and long-term discipline, it becomes evident that intelligent investing is never purely mechanical. It reflects how we perceive the world, what we value, and, most importantly, what we consider a life well lived. Money is not the destination; it is the mirror. And a portfolio, when truly understood, maps belief as much as it measures wealth.

The idea that there is a single "magic number" at which fulfilment arrives is among the most seductive—and corrosive—myths in contemporary finance. A million, five million, "just enough to be comfortable." The number drifts endlessly because it was never the source of security in the first place. The critical question is not whether your ETF allocation is optimised; it is whether your investments genuinely serve a life you recognise as meaningful. When enough is genuinely enough, the problem ceases to be numerical. It becomes ethical, even existential. This chapter begins there—by examining the shape of modern striving and how ETF investing can restore a more intentional relationship with sufficiency.

True wealth is seldom captured on balance sheets. It resides in the quality of your hours rather than the quantity of holdings. It is time autonomy, the freedom to decline, the capacity to work with integrity, to be present with those you love, to pursue ideas or causes unbound by commercial urgency. These are not ephemeral ambitions; they are the foundation of why financial independence matters. A portfolio is only meaningful if it sustains a well-lived life, which demands better questions than "How much did I beat the market by this year?" ETF investing, as we will see, can help cultivate that reorientation—less noise, less churn, more clarity.

Central to this discussion is the notion of stewardship. Not as a buzzword, but as a guiding identity. The steward-investor does not chase thrills or pursue alpha at any cost. They tend to a system. They understand that compounding—financial or otherwise—flourishes in fertile ground, not frenetic activity. Stewardship entails patience, responsibility, and a perspective that extends beyond the self. Whether managing £10,000 or £10 million, adopting a stewardship mindset changes how one engages with money. It directs focus from extraction to cultivation, from accumulation to alignment.

This lens also reshapes the concept of risk. Conventional finance asks, "How do I minimise risk to my capital?" but rarely, "What risk does this pose to my character, my family, my attention?" Portfolio management becomes a richer discipline when it includes the stewardship of the self. It is not only what you invest in, but how the investment process shapes who you become. Are you more anxious, distracted, reactive—or more grounded, focused, connected? These are not abstract musings; they are the invisible returns—or costs—of financial behaviour. ETFs, owing to their simplicity and transparency, provide a uniquely low-friction means to align investment with values—but only if you are attentive to the signals that truly matter.

This chapter also revisits the idea of the portfolio as philosophy. Each fund you hold represents a vote on how the world ought to operate. Do your holdings reflect resilience, sustainability, inclusive participation? Or are they tethered to narratives you would not endorse elsewhere in life? ESG debates aside, this is not a matter of moral perfection; it is about coherence. Do your financial structures amplify the kind of world you wish to inhabit? Do your time, money, and energy move in synchrony?

To be clear, this is not an exercise in abstraction. It is a return to fundamentals. Once the mechanics are in place—ETFs chosen, contributions automated, rebalancing scheduled—the substantive work begins. Not the tinkering, but the orientation. Measuring progress not by indices but by the fidelity of your days. This is the mature phase of investing: discipline integrated rather than reactive, and the measure not merely "Am I growing my capital?" but "Is this helping me live rightly?"

You will also encounter a critique of unbridled optimisation. The habit of tweaking every variable—portfolio, schedule, strategy—for peak efficiency can become an intellectual prison. Attention narrows to the measurable, the gamified: which ETF has the lowest fee, which tilt maximises the Sharpe ratio. These questions matter—but they are not sufficient. We advocate for an approach that values margin, spaciousness, and permission to stop incessantly tinkering. An investment plan that works with humanity, not against it.

Ultimately, this chapter reminds us that money, though potent, is a tool. Like all tools, it should not dictate the shape of life. ETF investing, when wielded thoughtfully, restores agency—not to hoard, but to design days deliberately. It is a means to an end. And that end is not simply financial independence, but congruence: the alignment of resources with values, action with belief.

Thus, the final question is not merely how to build wealth, but how to carry it. How to approach investing as an economic, moral, and philosophical practice. How to ensure your portfolio, calendar, and conversations mirror the person you are becoming and the world you aspire to support.

This is not the conclusion. It is the point at which the conversation deepens.

When Enough Is Truly Enough:

The most dangerous number in personal finance is the next one. A little more. Another ten percent. One more milestone. For many investors, especially those disciplined enough to build a well-structured ETF portfolio, the original goal—financial security, autonomy, peace of mind—is gradually displaced by a less definable but more intoxicating metric: *more.* This quiet drift is rarely planned. It is absorbed from headlines, peer comparisons, or the subtle pull of achievement addiction. The paradox is clear: *wealth, well managed, should create freedom.* But unchecked, it becomes a treadmill—exchanging one form of scarcity for another, cloaked in abundance.

This chapter challenges the assumption that investing is an endless game. It suggests that beyond a certain point, wealth ceases to be primarily functional and becomes psychological, even philosophical. The practical vehicle—low-cost, globally diversified ETFs—provides efficiency, clarity, and compounding over time. But these tools are only as effective as the mindset behind them. And without a calibrated sense of *enough*, the investor's tools may inadvertently reinforce the very anxiety they were meant to soothe.

The financial world rarely encourages sufficiency. Most content, platforms, and advisors are incentivised to promote movement: buying, rebalancing, optimising, growing. Very few ask whether the destination has already been reached—or whether continued striving might be diminishing returns in disguise. The concept of "enough" is therefore radical in a system designed for endless accumulation. It requires not merely restraint, but self-awareness. Not just asset allocation, but life allocation. *What is the wealth for?* If that question feels uncomfortable, it's precisely where clarity begins.

We must acknowledge that "enough" cannot be defined solely by spreadsheet logic. A £1 million portfolio may represent sufficiency for one investor and insecurity for another, depending on lifestyle needs, family obligations, personality traits, or past financial trauma. That doesn't make the concept subjective in a weak sense—it makes it personal in the strongest one. Wealth planning is not only a question of *what you can afford*, but *what you want to afford*. And perhaps even more deeply, *what you no longer need to chase.*

One of the practical strengths of ETF investing is how it simplifies the machinery of wealth-building. By automating contributions, reducing fees, and minimising behavioural errors, it creates space—intellectually and emotionally—for reflection. There is less friction, less noise, and fewer distractions. That space can be uncomfortable, especially for high-achieving individuals who are used to striving as default. But it's in that space that a different kind of decision-making becomes possible. ETF investing is not just efficient—it's clarifying. *It reveals when more activity is no longer necessary.* And that's when the question of "enough" becomes not only relevant, but urgent.

Consider a real-world example: a mid-career professional in her late 40s who has been investing steadily through ETFs for 15 years. She has no debt, a solid emergency fund, and a globally diversified portfolio worth £850,000. Every financial model she runs shows that, barring catastrophe, she could retire comfortably within a decade—possibly earlier with modest adjustments. But instead of satisfaction, she feels an intensifying pressure to reach £1.5 million. Why? Not because her expenses demand it. Not because she plans to dramatically expand her lifestyle. But because the number feels *safer*. And the market narrative around her rewards reaching for it. The problem is not mathematical—it's philosophical. She hasn't paused to ask: *What would change if I had more? And what am I postponing by chasing it?*

The idea of "the next number" functions like a mirage. It recedes as we approach. And unless interrupted, it displaces deeper questions about how we want to live. ETF investing offers an antidote not because it limits wealth creation, but because it makes enough visible. Once a long-term plan is in motion, growth becomes quieter, less eventful. That's the moment investors must learn to sit with sufficiency—*not* because ambition is wrong, but because unchecked ambition can erode satisfaction.

There is also a hidden cost to striving that goes beyond opportunity cost. Time, energy, and attention are finite. If an investor spends their most vibrant years optimising a future they never define, they risk building a structure they never fully inhabit. The point of long-term investing is *not* to defer living until some mythical net worth is reached. It is to build a financial framework that allows one to live with increasing alignment now. Every extra year of unnecessary accumulation is also a year delayed in doing something else—whether it's creative, relational, or spiritual.

This invites a reframing: wealth is not just a resource—it's a relationship. A relationship with possibility, yes, but also with fear, identity, and expectation. The investor who never questions their threshold for enough is not managing wealth—they're being managed by it. And markets, by their nature, will always offer reasons to delay satisfaction. Recessions, rallies, forecasts, and news cycles all conspire to unsettle the sense of arrival. That's why defining "enough" is not a one-time exercise—it's a discipline. And a rare one.

What role do ETFs play in all of this? Precisely because they resist drama. They do not promise outperformance. They do not tempt with fads. They do not require constant intervention. They are, in a sense, the investing equivalent of minimalist architecture—designed for function, clarity, and durability. And like minimalist design, they force a different conversation: *What truly adds value here? What would be enough?* For the investor willing to listen, ETFs are not just cost-effective—they are philosophically instructive.

There's also a moral dimension to sufficiency that rarely enters the financial dialogue. Every pound allocated toward unexamined accumulation is a pound not directed toward purpose. That could mean philanthropy, community investment, or simply the decision to work less and mentor more. When investors declare their "enough," they free up not only personal bandwidth, but societal capital. The ripple effect is non-trivial. Financial maturity is not just personal discipline—it's ecological in its impact.

This does not mean abandoning goals, ignoring risk, or ceasing to plan. It means clarifying what the wealth is *in service of*. Is it security? Time freedom? Creative latitude? Intergenerational support? Once that purpose is named, investment decisions become easier, not harder. You are not comparing ETF returns to headlines. You are comparing them to *needs*. And if the needs are already met, your work is no longer maximisation—it is stewardship.

Knowing when to stop is one of the most underdeveloped muscles in personal finance. Markets don't reward it. Media doesn't promote it. Advisors rarely teach it. But it may be the single most important skill for investors with a long time horizon and a well-constructed plan. ETFs offer the scaffolding. Only reflection can provide the signal. If the architecture of your portfolio is sound, then perhaps the final question is not "What's next?" but "What can I now say no to?"

Enough is not a ceiling. It is a design principle. It is the point where investing transforms from a pursuit into a practice—a quiet, confident stewardship of what already sustains you. Not less ambition, but better ambition. Not an end to growth, but a redefinition of where growth is needed most.

And so we close this section with a provocation: If your ETF plan is on track, if your expenses are covered, if your time is increasingly your own—what would you do differently if you believed that you had *enough*?

Let that be the metric that matters most.

Wealth as Relationship, Not Just Resource:

Wealth, for many, begins as a target—an amount, a figure, a goal on a spreadsheet. But for those who live with it long enough, it eventually reveals itself as something far more textured: a relationship. Numbers in isolation carry no wisdom. It is what they enable, reflect, or distort in our lives that gives them meaning. And so the question must evolve: *Not how much do you have, but how does what you have shape the way you live, choose, and connect?* Until wealth is understood relationally—not merely as a static resource—we risk letting it organise our lives by default, rather than design.

At its most mature, financial wealth is not simply stored purchasing power—it is a container for values. It expresses how we view time: whether we feel free or chronically rushed. It colours our relationship with work: whether it's pursued as obligation, craft, or escape. It spills into our presence with family: do we feel available, distracted, generous, transactional? And it inevitably shapes how we approach purpose: whether we build our days around meaning or margin. These aren't secondary concerns—they are the quiet outcomes of financial decisions repeated over decades. Wealth is never passive. Even when not being spent, it is shaping you.

Consider the way people talk about financial independence. Often, the language is mechanical—withdrawal rates, safe spending rules, portfolio sustainability. But very little is said about *what happens to the self* once autonomy is achieved. If your identity has been forged around accumulation, how do you inhabit rest? If your purpose has been productivity, what happens in stillness? A healthy relationship with wealth requires a capacity for these transitions. Without it, investors may achieve every financial milestone and still find themselves anxious, restless, or bored. Money can protect—but it cannot animate. That part must come from a deeper understanding of what it's *for.*

This brings us to the discipline of intentionality. In relationships with people, we recognise the importance of attention, care, and dialogue. In our relationship with wealth, we must cultivate the same. Too often, money becomes invisible until it is scarce—or excessive. But like any relationship left unattended, this neglect breeds misalignment. The investor who never stops to ask how their growing wealth is affecting their choices may wake up one day living a life shaped more by inertia than intention. The antidote is not more spreadsheets—it is reflection. How has money changed your habits, your friendships, your sense of risk, your sense of time? How much do you trust yourself with abundance? These are not financial questions. They are human ones.

ETF investing, for all its technical elegance, also plays a philosophical role here. Its simplicity allows for disconnection from the theatre of markets. It replaces adrenaline with patience, noise with structure. By taking decisions out of the daily spotlight, ETFs grant the investor space to ask deeper questions: *What do I want to be available for? What trade-offs am I no longer willing to make? What does spaciousness feel like when I stop confusing it with idleness?* In this sense, ETF investing is not just a tactic—it is an orientation. It suggests that peace of mind can be engineered, not through precision timing, but through relational clarity.

Wealth that is viewed only as resource will be managed, hoarded, optimised, and endlessly compared. Wealth that is experienced as relationship, by contrast, will be stewarded, shared, re-evaluated, and integrated. This is not merely semantics—it is the difference between anxiety and alignment. When wealth is seen as external to the self, it must constantly be defended or increased. When it is seen as part of one's expression, it becomes a medium for choices that resonate. A portfolio, in this view, is not a fortress—it is a mirror.

There is an ethical dimension to this as well. Wealth shapes our behaviour even when it isn't consciously guiding our actions. Research has repeatedly shown that financial security can increase empathy and generosity—but it can also breed insulation, complacency, and detachment. Which path is taken depends less on net worth than on mindset. The investor who views their assets as a tool for connection—supporting causes, enabling time-rich relationships, or mentoring others—will likely experience wealth as a life-enhancer. But the one who sees it as a moat, a scoreboard, or a permanent shield from vulnerability may find it corrosive, however large the account balance. *What you hold is less important than how it holds you.*

Take the example of a tech entrepreneur who exits their company with £3 million in invested ETFs by age 42. They have enough to live without ever working again. But they soon realise they've built their identity around hyper-productivity. In the absence of deadlines, they feel disoriented. Their wealth has bought them optionality—but not clarity. The mistake wasn't in how they invested. It was in never examining the identity beneath the money. They thought they were building financial independence. In truth, they were deferring the harder work of *personal* independence. The result is the same dilemma that haunts many high-achievers: wealth as armour, not as aliveness.

Contrast that with another case: a schoolteacher who invested steadily into a global ETF portfolio over 30 years, never earning more than £50,000 annually. At retirement, she has £600,000—modest by some standards, transformative by others. But she is clear: her money exists to support time with grandchildren, continued volunteer work, and the freedom to travel without financial anxiety. Her lifestyle is simple, but intentional. Her wealth is not a source of pressure, but permission. The relationship is one of trust, not tension. And that difference is qualitative, not numerical.

To reframe wealth as relationship is to ask better questions: How does my money affect my decisions, my time, and my emotional climate? What does it allow me to say *yes* to? What does it allow me to *decline* without fear? What does it reveal about what I truly value? These questions cannot be answered by portfolio dashboards alone.

They require self-awareness, curiosity, and the humility to revise old narratives. They ask the investor to integrate financial thinking with emotional intelligence, philosophical grounding, and ethical presence.

This reframe also invites investors to treat wealth less as a fixed state and more as a living practice. Just as one must revisit the dynamics of a relationship over time—adapting to seasons, crises, and growth—so too must our understanding of wealth evolve. The purpose of a £50,000 portfolio at age 28 is not the same as a £1.2 million portfolio at 55. Nor should it be. Static definitions of success betray the living, adaptive nature of a meaningful life. ETFs offer continuity. But the meaning of that continuity is up to the investor to define, refine, and—when necessary—release.

And this is where the power lies. When wealth is understood as relationship, the investor is no longer reactive to markets or external noise. They are attuned to internal alignment. They are less driven by metrics and more guided by values. They are able to decouple satisfaction from scale. And they are far more likely to experience their financial life not as a series of disconnected transactions—but as a coherent expression of who they are and what they care about.

The ETF investor, then, is not simply building a portfolio. They are building a life. A life where time has texture, relationships have room, and money becomes a servant to purpose—not a master of it. This is not sentimentalism. It is realism, matured. It is what emerges when wealth stops being a finish line and becomes a form of authorship.

That's the relationship worth cultivating.

The Investor as Steward:

There is a quiet but profound shift happening in how thoughtful individuals approach the act of investing. For decades, the dominant narrative cast the investor as a competitor—someone whose success was measured against indices, rivals, or time itself. Speed, strategy, and sharpness were the virtues that defined this archetype. Yet, this framing—borrowed from gamesmanship and speculation—often ignores a more enduring, holistic role: that of the steward. A steward does not chase; they tend. They do not conquer; they cultivate. They see wealth not merely as a personal tool, but as a shared resource to be maintained wisely and handed on responsibly. Investing, viewed through this lens, becomes less about extraction and more about care.

This reimagining of the investor is not abstract. It has deep philosophical and practical implications. Stewardship implies continuity. It requires patience, foresight, and a relationship to the future that goes beyond quarterly returns. When one thinks as a steward, every investment decision is laced with ethical dimension: *What am I endorsing? What am I enabling? What am I leaving behind?* These are not peripheral questions—they sit at the heart of responsible capital allocation. And they reveal that ETF investing, often dismissed as passive, can be anything but disengaged. When approached with intentionality, ETFs become an elegant vehicle for stewardship—broad-based, diversified exposure that reduces risk while quietly funding the infrastructure, institutions, and innovations we wish to endure.

Consider the structural difference between a speculative trader and a stewardship-oriented investor. The trader asks: *What will outperform this week?* The steward asks: *What will contribute enduring value over a generation?* These are not simply different timeframes—they are different worldviews. The trader is trying to outwit the market. The steward is trying to align with it—while directing capital toward systems that matter. In this sense, stewardship is not naïve idealism. It is pragmatism extended into responsibility. It says: if capital shapes the world, then I ought to care about where mine flows.

This orientation does not preclude returns. It deepens them. Financial performance is not sacrificed by thinking relationally. On the contrary, the stewardship mindset often leads to greater resilience. Investors who are committed to long-term sustainability tend to avoid short-term fads, resist panic selling, and remain anchored during volatility. They build portfolios that are designed to endure—not just in market cycles, but in moral coherence. That coherence, over time, becomes a stabiliser. It reduces regret. It fosters clarity. And it reinforces the idea that investing is not just a technical craft, but a moral one.

The shift toward stewardship also demands an awareness of *what* is being invested in—not just structurally, but socially. For instance, owning a broad-market ETF like one tracking the MSCI World Index may offer diversification, but it also reflects a cross-section of global corporate practices. Some of those practices may align with your values. Others may not. The steward pays attention. They don't need to screen every holding obsessively, but they do understand the directional flow of their capital. Is it enabling extractive industries, or funding renewable ones? Is it supporting companies that foster equitable workplaces, or merely chasing margin? These are not trivial questions. They are reflections of a deeper stance: that investing is, at its core, an act of participation in the systems we inhabit.

This participatory lens changes the investor's relationship to power. Instead of seeing themselves as removed observers—merely responding to market data—they become co-shapers of reality. Through ETFs, pensions, index funds, and ownership structures, private investors collectively influence the fate of institutions. Stewardship asks them to take that influence seriously. Voting proxies, for example—often ignored by retail investors—become opportunities to support better governance. Choosing ESG-aligned or socially screened ETFs, while imperfect, becomes an act of directional intent. Even divestment, where appropriate, becomes a form of moral signalling. The steward does not seek purity. They seek progress. They act, not to be flawless, but to be faithful to what they believe investment *ought* to support.

Stewardship is also intensely personal. It calls forth a slower, more reflective pace of decision-making. It resists the dopamine loop of daily price-checking and headline chasing. The steward builds a portfolio not just to protect themselves, but to honour what they have received—and to prepare something worthy to hand on. For those with children, this may take the form of intergenerational planning. For those without, it may involve philanthropy, legacy funding, or mentorship. But the thread remains the same: wealth is not hoarded; it is handed forward. Stewardship is the practice of turning accumulation into contribution.

Consider a family that chooses to invest in a global ETF portfolio structured to generate modest, sustainable returns over multiple decades. Rather than focusing on aggressive growth or market timing, they prioritise stability, diversification, and transparency. They discuss their investment approach openly with their children—not just the mechanics, but the values behind the strategy. They explain why they prefer low-cost funds, why they avoid certain sectors, and what principles guide their rebalancing. In doing so, they are not just managing money—they are modelling citizenship. They are showing that wealth, when approached with clarity and care, can support flourishing lives without dominating them.

Contrast this with the absentee investor—someone who outsources every decision, disengages from the consequences of their capital, and thinks only in terms of price appreciation. While their portfolio may grow, their understanding of its role in the world shrinks. Stewardship offers an antidote to this detachment. It invites ongoing engagement. It says: be curious, be attentive, and be accountable. You are not separate from the system in which your capital circulates. You are a participant—whether you admit it or not.

ETF investing, with its transparency and broad access, is uniquely suited to this model. It encourages long-termism by design. It discourages unnecessary churn. And it allows even modest investors to express conviction at scale. By owning a slice of the global economy, the ETF investor can support institutions that matter, while avoiding the hyper-concentration risks that come from stock-picking or trend-chasing. This is not about minimising effort—it is about maximising alignment. And alignment, in stewardship, is everything.

There is also a psychological transformation that occurs when the investor embraces stewardship. The anxiety of trying to outsmart the market gives way to the calm of contributing to it. The desperation for high-frequency wins is replaced by the satisfaction of meaningful progress. Time itself shifts from being an adversary to being an ally. And investment decisions begin to feel less like gambles and more like commitments. This is not just a change in technique. It is a shift in identity—from consumer to curator, from player to partner.

Stewardship also teaches a crucial truth often ignored in finance: *you cannot master what you do not love.* To be a good steward of one's wealth is to be in a respectful, ongoing relationship with it. This does not mean obsessing over returns or micromanaging allocations. It means paying attention, learning, revising, and remaining humble. It means remembering that financial systems are human systems—flawed, evolving, and open to influence. The steward does not retreat from complexity. They meet it with care.

Ultimately, stewardship invites the investor to ask a bigger question: *What am I really growing?* A portfolio? Certainly. But also a life. A sense of responsibility. A practice of alignment. A readiness to be not just well-resourced, but well-rooted. The goal is not to become perfect investors. It is to become wise ones. The kind who know that wealth is not merely a number—but a means. A means to shape, to support, and to serve. That is the investor as steward. And that is a role worth growing into.

The Portfolio as Philosophy:

There comes a point in the arc of any serious investor's education when spreadsheets lose their power to inspire. Alpha, beta, Sharpe ratios, and standard deviations begin to feel like only half the truth—necessary, but incomplete. The numbers, precise and rational as they may be, fail to capture the deeper questions: What am I funding? What systems am I reinforcing? Is this portfolio aligned with the kind of world I want to see thrive? These questions are not distractions from the investing process—they are the foundation of a more complete practice. Every financial decision, once stripped of abstraction, is ultimately a vote. A portfolio is not simply a bundle of securities; it is a personal philosophy expressed in capital allocation. The act of investing, especially when done passively through ETFs, may feel distant and dispassionate, but the implications of those choices ripple through economies, communities, and ecosystems. To see a portfolio only as a mechanism for compound growth is to miss the opportunity to see it as a form of agency—quiet but consequential.

The idea that finance is purely mechanical, separate from ethics or intention, has long been embedded in the dominant frameworks of modern portfolio theory. Risk is modelled as volatility. Optimisation assumes rational actors. Market participants are abstracted into datapoints. But real-world investing is messier, more human. When an investor chooses to overweight energy, or underweight emerging markets, or tilt toward ESG funds—they are expressing more than a preference for returns. They are revealing a worldview. Some do so consciously, others by default. But the expression is there, nonetheless. *Silence in investing is not neutrality; it is acquiescence.* Choosing a global index fund, for instance, implicitly supports a market-cap weighted vision of the world—one where scale equals relevance and economic might dominates moral deliberation. It's efficient, yes, but it's not ethically agnostic. That doesn't make it wrong. But it makes it worthy of scrutiny.

Consider the rise of thematic ETFs—vehicles that allow investors to focus on areas such as clean energy, cybersecurity, gender diversity, or artificial intelligence. These products are not just about chasing the next growth trend. For many investors, they serve as vehicles of alignment. They create coherence between personal conviction and portfolio construction. Of course, thematic investing is not immune to overreach. Many funds promise alignment without delivering substance. But at their best, these tools provide a bridge between belief and behaviour, enabling capital to flow toward what one deems meaningful. They remind us that markets do not merely reflect value—they shape it. By funnelling money into certain sectors, investors help set the tempo of innovation and the direction of development. An ETF is not just a mirror of the market. It is a lever, however small.

Yet thoughtful alignment does not require exclusionary zeal or ideological purity. Investing is not a religion. It is a dynamic act of trade-offs, weighed over time. To treat the portfolio as philosophy is not to insist on perfection. It is to replace passive default with active consideration. Even a simple global index investor, if self-aware, can make peace with the compromises embedded in their strategy. They may accept exposure to companies or regions they would not support individually, because they believe in the broader thesis of global growth. Or they may segment their portfolio—balancing a core of efficient exposure with satellite allocations to areas they want to support more directly. The key is not ideological coherence; it is intellectual honesty. *Know what your portfolio says about you—and be sure you want to be saying it.*

There is also a psychological dimension to this lens. When a portfolio feels aligned with purpose, it becomes easier to stick with it during volatile times. Investors often abandon strategy not because of losses alone, but because the pain lacks meaning. If a holding declines and you never truly believed in its role or story, the discomfort feels pointless. But if your portfolio reflects a thought-through worldview, setbacks feel like part of a longer arc. You are not merely enduring turbulence; you are holding a position with intention. This is not romanticism; it is a form of behavioural defence. *Alignment is discipline's ally.*

This perspective also reframes discussions of performance. Traditional investors ask, "How did this fund perform last quarter?" A more reflective investor might ask, "How did this allocation support the kind of world I care about building?" These are not mutually exclusive questions—but the latter adds depth to the former. It reminds us that there is more than one kind of return. Financial returns matter. But so does narrative coherence. So does social contribution. So does internal peace. The most powerful portfolios are not necessarily the ones that beat benchmarks every year. They are the ones that survive scrutiny, both external and internal.

None of this requires abandoning ETFs. In fact, ETFs can be powerful vehicles for alignment, precisely because of their diversity, accessibility, and specificity. They allow investors to build portfolios that reflect a complex set of values without the overhead of active stock-picking or individual speculation. One might choose a global low-carbon equity ETF to reflect environmental concern, pair it with a local municipal bond fund to support community infrastructure, and hold a broad-based index as a ballast. The result is not a static statement of virtue but a living, evolving philosophy—subject to review, responsive to learning, and humble before uncertainty.

This approach also demands a shift in what we measure. The investor-as-philosopher is less obsessed with short-term relative returns and more attuned to long-term resonance. Does this portfolio help me sleep at night? Does it make sense in light of my personal priorities? Does it reflect the best of what I believe about humanity's potential—or merely mimic what's easy and available? These are not soft questions. They are rigorous. They require courage to ask and patience to answer. And they demand that we take responsibility for what our money does when we are not watching.

As passive investing continues to dominate flows and index funds shape the contours of global capital, the question of intention becomes more—not less—important. It is easy to hide behind low fees and efficient exposure. It is harder to interrogate the assumptions baked into those indices. Who benefits from the current structure? Whose voice is reflected in the weighting? What innovations are being subsidised or neglected? These are not theoretical exercises. They are essential tools for conscious participation.

In closing—not to wrap the argument, but to centre it—we must remember that wealth is not just what we accumulate; it is what we accelerate. A portfolio is a force, not just a container. It has direction, consequence, and character. To treat it as merely a set of financial instruments is to miss its expressive power. The investor is not a bystander. They are a shaper. And their portfolio is not just a map of their money—it is a portrait of their mind. That is the opportunity. That is the responsibility. And that is why investing, when done with eyes open and values engaged, is not just a tactic for prosperity. It is a philosophy in motion.

Conclusion
Stillness in Motion

There is a peculiar calm that follows clarity. Not the hollow pause of indecision, but the steady quiet of knowing. It is the hush that descends once complexity has been distilled—not into slogans or glib shortcuts, but into something more enduring: conviction unaccompanied by noise. This chapter does not aim to furnish new arguments or technical refinements. Instead, it marks a deliberate slowing, a turning inward, a final meditation on the kind of investor—and the kind of person—you are becoming.

Throughout the preceding chapters, we have constructed a framework for ETF-based investing rooted in clarity, intentionality, and strategic composure. Markets have been treated not as arenas for speculation but as landscapes to be navigated with reasoned care. Volatility has been reframed, not as a menace, but as a feature to be harnessed. Performance has been redefined to encompass discipline, patience, and peace of mind. And the portfolio has been presented as more than a ledger of returns—as a reflection of values. Now, at the close of this journey, the question deepens: what remains when the noise is stripped away?

Modern investing is loud by design. It rewards motion, sensationalises change, and thrives on urgency masquerading as insight. Alerts ping, headlines flare, charts flicker—all conspiring to instil the sense that inertia is failure. This chapter challenges that assumption. It argues that the truest measure of financial competence lies not in constant optimisation, but in sustained composure. The ability to hold—to remain invested through seasons of doubt, distraction, and disruption—is not passivity; it is strength. Stillness, in the right context, is not absence of motion—it is control in motion.

Remaining still in markets demands more than technical expertise; it requires personal transformation. A shift from reaction to reflection is essential. This chapter begins there—not with strategies, but with questions investors seldom ask themselves: What is enough—for you, not anyone else? Which risks are real, and which are mere theatre? Are you shaping your life around your investments, or are your investments shaping your life? These are not idle thoughts—they are instruments of focus, shields against behavioural traps that can undermine even the most meticulous portfolio.

Stillness does not equate to stagnation, nor is it an excuse for disengagement. On the contrary, it emerges from diligent upfront work: clarifying objectives, selecting instruments with care, automating contributions and rebalancing, and then permitting those systems to operate without constant interference. It entails cultivating a healthy indifference to short-term fluctuations and a deep attachment to long-term processes. Stillness is achieved when the architecture of your investing life is sturdy enough that revisiting decisions is unnecessary—unless the world, or your values, genuinely change.

Yet one form of motion this chapter encourages wholeheartedly is reflection. Not motion for its own sake, but considered thought as a pathway to maturity. Prompts, rather than prescriptions, guide this practice: what did you feel during your first trade? Where were you tempted to act emotionally, and what did resisting that impulse teach you? Which holdings feel misaligned with your present self? Which continue to serve the person you are becoming? Journaling these reflections creates a private ledger—not of transactions, but of insight. Over time, it charts intellectual and emotional evolution in a way that may prove more valuable to your long-term net worth than any quarterly performance report.

The chapter also looks ahead. The work is never finished: markets shift, life changes, and the tools at our disposal evolve. Yet core principles—simplicity, intentionality, reflection—remain the most enduring assets. To sustain this, a roadmap for lifelong learning is offered. Not a syllabus or credential, but a mental model: stay curious, revisit your assumptions, and return to first principles when confusion arises. A financially literate adult is not defined by the latest terminology or trend, but by the capacity to learn, adapt, and regain calm amidst complexity.

Perhaps most importantly, this chapter reminds us that investing is not about "winning" in financial terms. It is about living more fully, with less fear. An investor who no longer panics during market downturns is not simply disciplined—they have begun to sever their sense of security from external noise. Such transformation ripples beyond spreadsheets: it reshapes work, time, legacy, and relationships. It enables questions that matter: not "Will I have enough?" but "What do I wish to be free to do?" Not "How do I beat the market?" but "How do I live meaningfully?"

Ultimately, this book offers more than a system for wealth creation; it provides a lens for rethinking money itself. Money is neither the destination nor merely a tool. It is a mirror, reflecting the depth of our self-understanding and the clarity of our values. Investing through ETFs—strategically, calmly, reflectively—is not about outwitting the world. It is about aligning with it on your terms: process over prediction, principle over impulse, substance over flash.

This chapter, then, is not a conclusion. It is an invitation: to pause, to clarify, to continue. To safeguard the simplicity you have cultivated and defend it against the forces that would distract or dilute it. Let others chase trends, panic, sell, and restart. You, now, are anchored. Not because you know everything, but because you know enough.

And in that knowing, you have achieved more than most ever do.

Final Reflection:

The final test of any investing philosophy is not how loudly it performs in a bull market, nor how cunningly it hedges in a bear one. It's not the sharpness of its charts or the cleverness of its metrics. The true test is quieter: Does it help you sleep at night? Does it help you live better during the day? A well-constructed investment life, like a well-built home, eventually fades into the background. It supports without demanding attention. It steadies without spectacle. This final section is about that rare and understated form of success—*a state of stillness that isn't idle, but complete.*

In a culture wired for acceleration—more trades, more data, more commentary—it is radical to stop and ask: what if I've done enough? Financial stillness does not mean refusing to learn or ignoring changing circumstances. Rather, it means *choosing not to overreact in the face of them.* It is the practice of anchoring your decisions in principle rather than prediction. And over time, it produces something even more valuable than compounding capital: a steady mind.

The temptation to tinker never fully disappears. New ETFs launch. New trends emerge. New tax rules, market forecasts, geopolitical events—all feed the background hum of uncertainty. There is always something to update, reconsider, adjust. And yet, past a certain point, most of this energy is wasted. A good plan, well-executed and patiently held, outperforms the majority of frantic attempts to game the system. What most investors need is not more movement, but better mental posture. *Discipline is not about gritting your teeth. It is about removing the need to grit them in the first place.*

This section is a meditation on the power of that mental stillness—not as an abstract virtue, but as a hard-earned result of clarity, systems, and self-awareness. We revisit the architecture of a sound portfolio not to tweak its mechanics, but to understand its emotional utility. The goal is not just to build wealth. The goal is to become the kind of person who is no longer *afraid of the future.* Someone who can absorb uncertainty without abandoning reason. Someone who can hear noise and not mistake it for signal. Someone who, having defined what *enough* looks like, stops chasing more and starts living more fully.

Clarity of this kind is rare. It takes time, and deliberate reflection. But it is worth cultivating. One way to begin is through structured self-inquiry. Consider the following questions—not as a checklist, but as invitations:

What role does money play in your sense of identity?
What fears drive your investment decisions, and are they justified?
Do your financial behaviours align with your stated values, or do they contradict them under pressure?
Have you defined what financial success actually looks like in your own life—not in abstract returns, but in real-life terms?

Are you preparing for a future you can visualise, or simply reacting to a world you fear?

These are not theoretical exercises. They shape how you react during moments of stress—when markets fall, headlines shout, or friends share their "wins." Investors who have done this reflective work do not panic when prices dip. They do not overextend during bull runs. They understand *what their money is for*, and that understanding acts as ballast during storms.

Financial media rarely encourages such thoughtfulness. Its incentives lie in urgency: the next hot sector, the latest Fed whisper, the headline that changes everything. But if you take even a short step back, it becomes obvious: this noise is a tax on your attention, not a source of clarity. The most useful information for a long-term investor is not what will happen tomorrow, but how to behave when tomorrow surprises you.

Stillness is not inaction. It is a cultivated form of restraint—an ability to act only when it matters and stay calm when it doesn't. And it is built, paradoxically, through consistent *motion* in one direction: contribution. That is why this chapter doesn't suggest sitting back, doing nothing, and hoping. Rather, it urges continued engagement, but with intention. Keep learning, yes—but in service of reinforcing your framework, not second-guessing it. Stay informed, but selectively. Rebalance when needed, but not out of boredom. Simplicity is not laziness. It is the result of thoughtful pruning.

Simplicity also preserves the most undervalued asset in finance: *attention*. Every article you don't read, every trade you don't place, every opinion you choose not to internalise—these are not omissions. They are investments in your future mental bandwidth. They keep you focused on the handful of things that truly matter: your savings rate, your asset allocation, your time horizon, your behaviour.

If there is a roadmap for life after this book, it's not a prescriptive list of next steps. It's a mindset. Curiosity without frenzy. Learning without anxiety. Confidence without rigidity. Your ETF portfolio may be built on indexes, but your investing life is built on perspective. You are not optimising for headlines. You are optimising for *longevity*—of wealth, of wellbeing, and of clarity.

That longevity benefits from periodic reflection. Not as a performance review, but as a calibration tool. What assumptions did you hold that proved wrong—and why? What worked surprisingly well? Where did emotion nearly sabotage good judgement? This kind of self-audit is not about shame or ego. It's about refinement. The investors who improve over time are not the ones with the best forecasts, but the ones with the best feedback loops.

So much of investing advice focuses on technique—allocations, tax wrappers, factor tilts. All useful. But what shapes your outcomes most is not strategy. It's temperament. And temperament is shaped by how you relate to time. Stillness is the art of being in time without being pushed by it. Of letting compounding work without forcing it. Of trusting your process enough to give it air. *Patience, in a world trained to sprint, is a form of rebellion.*

This brings us to a final point—perhaps the most important in this entire volume. A good investing life is not just about markets. It is about *meaning*. If all this work—the research, the automation, the resisting of noise—is done solely to amass more digits on a screen, then something vital has been missed. Wealth is not a scoreboard. It is a tool. And like all tools, its value depends on how wisely and humanely it is used.

Wealth, when well managed, should create space: for relationships, for purpose, for time used intentionally rather than reactively. The final test of an ETF strategy—or any strategy—is whether it leaves you more present, more grounded, more capable of generosity and calm. It should make you not just richer, but better.

That is the stillness we hope to leave you with. Not a silence of ignorance or avoidance, but a quiet born of alignment. A life where investing no longer feels like a contest, but a craft. Where simplicity is not a compromise, but a triumph. Where enough is not a ceiling, but a choice.

This is not the end. It is a handover. From this book to your life. From theory to practice. From learning to living.

You are ready.

About the Author

Julian Raye writes about money the way others write about philosophy—calmly, precisely, and with quiet conviction. With over a decade immersed in global markets and personal finance systems, he believes that investing should not feel like gambling or guesswork, but like tending a well-designed garden. Julian is deeply committed to reshaping how people relate to wealth—shifting the conversation from hype and hustle to structure, stillness, and stewardship. His writing blends strategic insight with psychological depth, empowering readers to build portfolios that reflect not only financial goals but personal values. When he's not writing or working with long-term investors, Julian is walking forest trails, rebalancing portfolios, and practicing the art of doing less—intentionally.

www.ingramcontent.com/pod-product-compliance
Lightning Source LLC
Chambersburg PA
CBHW031347230926
51848CB00002B/421
* 9 7 8 9 3 7 1 7 7 9 8 2 1 *